TRADITIONAL

BREAD
MAKING

TRADITIONAL

BREAD MAKING

Eve Parker

AURA

This edition published in 2012
by Baker & Taylor (UK) Limited,
Bicester, Oxfordshire

Copyright © 2012 Arcturus Publishing Limited
26/27 Bickels Yard, 151–153 Bermondsey Street
London SE1 3HA

ISBN: 978-1-90723-126-1
AD002226EN

Printed in China

CONTENTS

INTRODUCTION: Why Bake Your Own Bread? 6

GETTING STARTED 9
  Ingredients 10
  Equipment 19

THE TECHNIQUES 23
  Learning the Techniques 24
  Troubleshooting 34

THE CLASSICS 37

SPECIALITY BREADS 59

FLAT BREADS 81

GLUTEN-FREE BREADS 99

QUICK & SWEET BREADS 111

USING UP LEFTOVERS 149

INDEX 158

WHY BAKE YOUR OWN BREAD?

There is nothing quite like seeing your homemade loaf baking inside the oven, filling the kitchen with tantalizing fragrances. If you're one of those people who love that idea but feel intimidated by the mere thought of baking bread, you'll realize from this book just how easy it can be if you follow a few simple guidelines.

Today, many people take the humble loaf for granted, quickly grabbing a packaged version from the supermarket shelf without giving a second thought to the ingredients and flavour.

Yet bread deserves more respect, for its ancestry can be traced back as far as 8,000 years, to the days when tools were still made from stone and the oven was a simple flat rock placed over an open fire. Evidence from archaeological digs has shown that this bread was hard on the teeth, very different from the soft, pliable bread we know today. It was made from just flour and water; any form of leavening agent had yet to be discovered.

According to legend, the secret of leavened bread was first discovered in Ancient Egypt when a baker temporarily forgot about his dough and left it standing long enough to ferment. The final result was a much lighter, more palatable bread.

The Romans learned the technique from the Egyptians and it is believed that by the year 100BC there were as many as 250 bakers' shops in the city of Rome. However, when the Roman Empire collapsed in AD476, the secret of making leavened bread was lost and would not be rediscovered for many centuries.

Bread in England was usually made from a mixture of grains,

in particular barley and rye; only the upper classes could afford the expensive white bread made from wheat. Not until the 19th century did imported wheat become more readily available – but then parliament imposed heavy taxes on it, causing the price to rise and once again putting it out of the reach of most people.

The mass manufacture of bread as we know it today began in the 20th century, with products bearing little resemblance to the original domestic loaf. When you next reach for that mass-produced sliced loaf, remember the tradition of bread making through the centuries and perhaps consider taking a leaf from our predecessors' book and start baking our own.

A WAY TO UNWIND

As the pace of life seems to speed ever faster, many of us look for ways to unwind and take our minds off the stresses of everyday life. Some people turn to gardening and some to reading, while others find the simple pleasure of kneading dough a wonderful way to relax.

Of course, busy mothers and people who work full-time may prefer to use a bread-making machine, which will do the majority of the work. But this book is about making bread the traditional way. If you are really short of time, you can speed up the kneading process by using a food processor with a dough hook attachment. However, once you have learned the basics and found out just how enjoyable making bread can be, getting your hands covered in dough will seem the best part of the process.

BEING CREATIVE

Once you feel confident about making a basic loaf – and practice will indeed make perfect – you can start being creative. Not only can you experiment with different flavourings and textures, you can also try making different shapes, such as a round loaf or a long baguette. You may even feel like tackling a plaited loaf.

The art of bread making is fascinating, because just a few basic ingredients can be turned into hundreds of different types of bread. As you become more proficient, you'll find that a delicious, traditional fresh loaf will take pride of place on your

table – at breakfast, lunch and dinner! You'll soon experience pleasure in the care and time you have taken to make your bread and you will glow with pride when friends and family ask you where you bought that wonderful-tasting loaf!

Traditional Bread Making provides clear, thorough explanations in a simple step-by-step format. The introductory section, Getting Started, gives an overview of the equipment and the basic ingredients you need, while Part 2, The Techniques, teaches the art of kneading and punching down by hand. It explains why bread has to be left to prove (or rise) not just once but twice in most cases. This section will help you to avoid any pitfalls in your quest to create the perfect loaf.

Hopefully this book will whet your appetite and encourage you to embark upon a new and satisfyingly productive hobby. Happy baking!

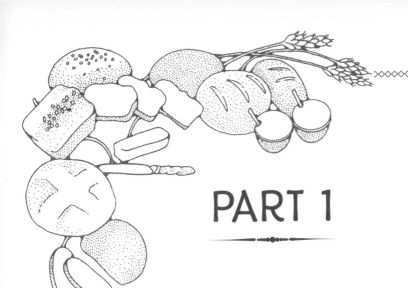

PART 1

GETTING STARTED

In the case of bread baking, knowledge is the all-important tool. Although only four basic ingredients are needed to make bread, it is vital to learn how they work together. The complex way in which they react with one another is paramount to the success of the end result.

INGREDIENTS

The main ingredients of bread are flour, yeast, water and salt.
Nothing could be simpler, you might think; but each of these
ingredients has a precise role to play before you can
create the perfect dough.

Your first job is to buy the basic ingredients. Their simplicity means that you won't have to make extra trips to speciality shops – they can all be purchased from your local supermarket. Having said that, once you are more experienced and wish to experiment with different types of flour, you may find you have to search a little harder.

To produce the perfect loaf you should buy the highest-quality ingredients that your purse will allow. These are, after all, the foundation to all the recipes and some of the cheaper flours will produce inferior dough. This section of the book describes the range of ingredients available to you and the way you can use

them to your best advantage.

One of the secrets to making great-tasting bread is time – without this you will end up with a mediocre loaf that won't have been worth the effort. Don't rush the kneading and proving stages, as these are vital to the fermentation process which is explained in the next few pages.

Follow the recipes carefully and make sure you weigh each ingredient accurately, otherwise you could end up with a heavy, unpalatable loaf.

The recipes in this book provide both metric and imperial measurements.

FLOUR

Flour is made by grinding grains such as barley, buckwheat, corn, rye and wheat into a fine powder. Wheat flour is the most usual type of bread-making flour in Europe. This is because it has a high gluten content which makes the dough lighter and more elastic than bread made from other flours (see box, right).

Wheat flours

There are six varieties of wheat: durum, hard red spring, hard red summer, hard white, soft red winter and soft white. When a wheat is referred to as 'hard', it means it contains a higher proportion of gluten to starch, which gives it more elasticity. You can purchase flour specially milled for bread baking which, because of its higher gluten content, will absorb more liquid. This type of dough also rises

GLUTEN

Flour contains two proteins called gliadin and glutenin which together form gluten. This is a strong, elastic substance which stretches and rises when it reacts with yeast or another raising agent. When you add water to flour, the gluten starts to swell and forms a continuous network of fine strands. Bread without gluten is not as light and porous, and has a much denser consistency than regular bread.

more than dough made from regular plain flour.

Granary flour This is a blend of different flours, usually wholemeal, white and rye. Its defining characteristic is the presence of malted wheat, which gives it a nutty flavour.

Plain flour Referred to as all-purpose flour in the USA, this is a blend of hard and soft wheats. Although it can be used in bread making, plain flour is more commonly used for baking cakes, biscuits and pastries because it has less gluten and is therefore less elastic than the stronger bread flours.

Self-raising flour This is a plain white flour to which a chemical raising agent such as baking powder has been added. While it's generally used for baking cakes, it can also be used in yeast-free breads.

Stoneground flour Traditionally produced by milling the wheat slowly between stones, this flour retains more of its natural flavours and nutrients than regular flour.

Strong flour Also known as bread flour, this is made from hard wheat and is specially milled for making bread.

Wheatmeal (brown) flour This is produced in the same way as wholemeal flour (see below) but does not have the same density of bran. The result is a lighter, less dense dough.

Wholemeal flour This is made from the whole wheat kernel. Because wholemeal flour has a high bran content, the finished loaf is dense and highly nutritious.

Other flours
The following flours work best when combined with wheat flours. People who are ready to experiment can use them to add texture and extra flavour.

Buckwheat flour In spite of its name, this grain is not related to wheat. The flour is greyish in colour, with a nutty flavour.

It makes an excellent wheat substitute for those with gluten intolerance, but is often mixed with other flours because it can have a bitter taste.

Corn flour Corn is ground to three different textures: coarse, medium and fine. The fine variety is generally used as a thickening agent for making sauces. Cornmeal, which is yellow in colour, is used to make Italian polenta but is not really suitable for making bread. All corn flours are gluten-free, so cornbread is suitable for those who are gluten intolerant.

Oatmeal This comes in various grades, from fine to pinhead. Mixed with other flours it can make a lovely nutty loaf. Some, but not all gluten-intolerant people can eat oats. It is still unclear whether oats contain gluten or whether gluten is introduced via cross-contamination with other grains during processing.

Rye flour Ground from the whole grain, rye flour produces very dense bread because it is low in gluten. When mixed with wheat flour, the result is a dense, dark, richly flavoured bread. It works well in sweet quick breads.

Spelt flour An ancient relative of modern-day wheat, spelt has a unique, nutty flavour. It has quite a high gluten content so is ideal for making bread. However, as it is lighter than normal wheat flour, people who are wheat intolerant may find it easier to digest.

RAISING AGENTS

The majority of the breads in this book are raised (or leavened) using yeast. In some of the quick breads, a chemical raising agent such as baking powder is used, while flat breads require no raising agent at all.

Yeast

Yeast is by far the most common raising agent used in bread

making. It is available in three forms: fresh, dried and easy-blend (see below). Yeast is a living organism which converts the natural sugars in flour into carbon dioxide, a gas that makes the bread rise. As yeast is very sensitive to heat, you need to ensure that the liquid you use in your recipe is at the correct temperature. The same is true of the place where you leave the dough to rise. If it is too cool, the yeast will be slow to activate, too hot and the yeast will die.

Dried yeast Also known as dried active yeast, this consists of tiny granules that must be dissolved in the liquid recommended in your recipe before being added to the flour. It has twice the strength of fresh yeast.

Easy-blend yeast This type of yeast can be mixed straight into the flour and is activated as soon as warm liquid is added to the bowl. It is also known as fast-action yeast.

Fresh yeast Although the recipes in this book all suggest the use of dried or easy-blend yeast for convenience, fresh yeast produces the best flavour and is easier to digest.

As fresh yeast is hard to track down in some places, it's best to use the dried forms to begin with. However, you might like to try using some fresh yeast once you have mastered the basics of bread making and are feeling more ambitious. Fresh yeast is available in a compressed form. It is 70 per cent liquid and therefore highly perishable (unlike dried active yeast which will keep for up to a year if stored in the refrigerator). Even if kept in the refrigerator, fresh yeast will deteriorate after two weeks. It can be stored successfully in the freezer to extend its life, but must be defrosted at room temperature and then used immediately.

Fresh yeast should be pale grey-brown in appearance, sweet-smelling, soft and crumbly. If there is any sign of mould on the surface, or if the yeast is beginning to harden, it should be discarded.

MAKING A STARTER

Until yeast became widely available, bakers used to make their own leavening agents, called 'starters', from wild yeast found naturally in the air. They did this by leaving a bowl of flour and warm water in the bakery to ferment for several days.

Many bakers today still use a starter with the addition of dried yeast because they find it produces a more reliable dough. Making your own starter requires some planning, but if you are happy to experiment you could find that the bread you make has a unique flavour.

One of the most reliable starters is sourdough; this originated in France, where it is called *levain*. If you follow the simple instructions here you should find you are rewarded with consistent results.

Making a sourdough starter

75g/2½oz + 2 tbsp white or
    wholemeal bread flour
120ml/4fl oz + 2 tbsp bottled water

1. Put 75g/2½oz flour and 120ml/ 4fl oz water in a large, very clean glass bowl and stir until thoroughly combined.
2. Cover the bowl with a piece of clean muslin secured with a piece of string or large elastic band. Leave at room temperature overnight.
3. The following morning, mix in a further 2 tablespoons of flour and 2 tablespoons of water. Cover again, leave to stand until the evening and then give it another stir.
4. Within 4–7 days, depending upon the surrounding temperature, the mixture should start to show bubbles and humidity. Don't worry if it separates in the first few days – this is quite normal.
5. Once the starter has been bubbling for at least 2–3 days it should have generated

enough wild yeast to make it suitable for use.

6. As long as you replace the same amount of flour and water each time you use your starter, the bacteria and yeast will naturally regulate themselves. If the starter begins to smell putrid, throw it away and begin afresh.

Chemical raising agents

This type of leavening agent was not discovered until the middle of the 19th century. Just like yeast, chemical raising agents such as baking powder produce carbon dioxide, but the reaction is swift so no proving time is required. The dough must be baked as soon as the bubbles start to appear as they rapidly lose their effectiveness.

Breads made using chemical raising agents go stale very quickly, so should be eaten on the day they are baked.

HYDRATION

You may come across the word 'hydration' in relation to bread dough. This is simply a baker's way of referring to the amount of water the dough contains. The following terms describe a dough's water content:

Stiff and dry – 58–60 per cent
Firm – 60–62 per cent
Modestly firm – 62–63 per cent
Malleable – 63–64 per cent
Soft – 64–65 per cent
Moist – 65–67 per cent

LIQUIDS

Whether you use water, milk, beer, buttermilk or even yoghurt, liquid is a vital component in bread making. Its first function, provided it is at the right temperature, is to activate the yeast; its second is to moisten the flour so that you can shape it into a dough.

Most people use water to make bread dough and tap water is perfectly adequate. To activate the yeast, the water must be around body temperature – 37°C/98.6°F. If you are not confident that you can guess this correctly, try using a thermometer. However, the easiest way to get the right temperature is to mix two-thirds cold water with one-third boiling water.

SALT

Even though salt is used in only very small quantities, it plays an important role in making bread. It is added to give the bread flavour, but more importantly it helps to control the fermentation process. Salt contributes to the chemical bonds in gluten by strengthening the network of strands; it also slightly retards the activity of the yeast. There are many types of salt to choose from, for example, fine sea salt, table salt or kosher salt. Coarse sea salt is not recommended for use, as the larger granules don't dissolve very easily in the dough.

Most bread recipes use approximately 2 per cent salt by weight; too much salt will drastically hinder the fermentation process. If you are mixing ingredients in advance of preparation, don't allow the salt to come into contact with the yeast as this can stop the fermentation process completely.

SUGAR

In the past sugar was essential to 'feed' the yeast, but modern yeasts don't require sugar to become active. However, a small amount of sugar, usually granulated, is still added to the dough even in savoury recipes, as it helps to enhance the flavour, add crispness to the crust and generally improve the texture of the dough. You can use alternative sweeteners, such as honey, molasses, and maple or golden syrup, to experiment with the different flavours. Like salt, sugar attracts water which means the bread will stay moist for longer than sugar-free dough.

FATS

Although fat should be used sparingly when making bread, it is an important ingredient because it moistens the bread, tenderizes the crumb and acts as a preservative. A typical French loaf, which contains no fat, will start to go stale as soon as it cools and has to be eaten on the day of baking. A dough containing some fat (rich dough), whether in the form of butter, oil, eggs, cream, milk, lard or solid vegetable shortening, will remain fresh for twice as long.

It doesn't matter whether you use solid fat or oil – they both produce the same effect, but the flavour will be completely different. Olive oil has a distinctive flavour of its own and is not an ideal substitute for butter, whereas vegetable oils, which are milder in flavour, are perfectly acceptable.

As long as solid fat is at room temperature when it is added, the kneading process will be enough to incorporate it into the dough. If you choose not to use butter, don't reach for the margarine as a substitute as it contains too much water. Instead use lard, as it gives the finished bread a lovely flaky texture and a wonderfully crisp crust. Solid vegetable shortening is the vegetarian alternative.

NEED TO KNOW

Use either butter or lard to grease your loaf tins – never margarine, as it can scorch the crust of your bread.

EQUIPMENT

You will find a tempting range of bread-making equipment in specialist cookery shops, but you don't need to break the bank to get started. What's important here is the personal touch you bring to your hand-made creation.

No piece of machinery, however sophisticated, can replicate the quality and flavour of a loaf made by hand. Even though the white, sliced, pre-packaged, almost tasteless sandwich loaf is convenient to use and stays fresh for ages (because it is full of preservatives), an increasing number of people today are shunning these mass-produced breads and having a go at making their own. This section discusses the basic equipment required and the role played by each item.

SCALES

It is vital that all ingredients are measured accurately, so scales are the most important piece of equipment you will need. Don't be tempted to guess quantities as you will be disappointed by the end result. The recipes in this book have been calculated to give you perfect results every time, so make sure you follow them carefully.

The most accurate scales are the digital type, which are easy to use and take up very little space in the kitchen compared to the more cumbersome balance scales. Digital scales have a tiny computer inside, so they can measure even the smallest amounts, and most of them can be used for weighing in either metric or imperial measurements.

When buying digital scales, make sure they have the function to return to '0'. For example, when you place an empty bowl on the scales, you will need to return the reading to '0' to weigh the flour and other ingredients accurately (without including the bowl itself).

US CUP MEASUREMENTS

You may find that many of your recipe books use US cup measurements. These are harder to convert than metric and imperial measurements, since dry goods are variable in terms of weight to volume. If you wish to make bread using US cups it's best to buy a set of cup measures, which are available at most kitchen shops. These will include teaspoon and tablespoon measures too, which differ from UK equivalents.

MEASURING SPOONS AND CUPS

Buy yourself a decent set of measuring spoons – just using a regular teaspoon or tablespoon is not a sufficiently reliable way to measure ingredients for bread. When filling the spoon, refrain from packing the ingredient too tightly. Level the ingredient off with the back of a knife. Don't rely on 'a pinch of salt', which works well in most recipes but not for baking bread.

To measure liquid, use a glass measuring jug with clearly marked increments on the side. For an accurate reading, place the jug on a flat surface and view the measurement at eye level.

ELECTRIC MIXER

Some home bakers like to use an electric mixer to take some of the work out of the kneading process. This is fine if you are really short of time, but this book aims to teach you the 'feel' of the dough so that you know when it has reached the optimum elasticity.

If you want to use a mixer, you will need to obtain a heavy-duty one with a dough hook attachment. Standard kitchen mixers with whisk or paddle attachments only are not strong enough to deal with heavy bread dough. The dough hook should have a complex bend to it, not just a curve; a straighter hook will take longer to knead the dough and result in a poor loaf. The mixer bowl should be at least 5 litres (8¾ pints), or it won't be large enough to handle the amount of dough used in most of these recipes.

Finally, always follow the manufacturer's instructions carefully when using your mixer.

BAKING MOULDS AND TINS

The best moulds and tins to buy are the non-stick variety, as they are easier to clean and the bread will be easier to remove after it is cooked. Try to acquire an assortment of sizes and shapes, remembering that the dough will almost double in size after the final proving.

As you start to experiment with some of the more complicated recipes, you may wish to purchase special moulds for brioches and baking trays for rolls, buns and croissants.

SCRAPERS

Plastic scrapers designed specifically for bread baking are handy tools. They range from flexible, curved plastic blades, designed for scraping the last pieces of dough out of the bowl, to long, straight-edged bench scrapers, which are sharpened slightly and useful for dividing the dough or scraping it off the work surface.

WIRE COOLING RACK

You will definitely need to buy a wire rack on which to rest the bread after its removal from the oven. Air needs to circulate around the bread while it cools, or else the loaf will go soggy.

TEA TOWEL

Keep a couple of clean tea towels handy to cover the dough during proving.

PROVING BOWLS OR TUBS

You will need large bowls or tubs to hold the dough while it is set aside to prove. Ideally these should be made of plastic, as this retains a neutral temperature that doesn't interfere with the natural fermentation process. Choose smooth-sided containers so that you can remove the dough easily once it has risen. Alternatively, placed the dough on a large wooden board and cover it with a clean tea towel.

BAKING PARCHMENT

Some of the recipes require you to use baking parchment to line the pans. This stops the dough from sticking to the pans and makes the bread easier to remove after baking. Parchment is usually bought on a roll and comes either bleached (white) or unbleached (natural).

PASTRY BRUSHES

Some of the more elaborate breads require a final wash or glaze before baking. This should be applied using a soft-bristled pastry brush so that you do not mark or damage the surface.

SHARP KNIFE

In some of the recipes you will need a sharp knife to score the surface of the loaf. If the blade is blunt it will drag on the dough and spoil the shape.

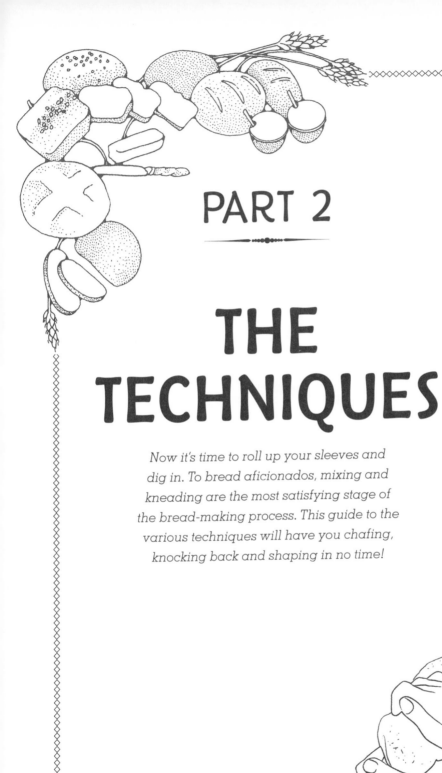

PART 2

THE TECHNIQUES

Now it's time to roll up your sleeves and dig in. To bread aficionados, mixing and kneading are the most satisfying stage of the bread-making process. This guide to the various techniques will have you chafing, knocking back and shaping in no time!

LEARNING THE TECHNIQUES

In this section you will learn about preparation, mixing,
kneading, proving, knocking back, dividing and shaping,
cooking, storing and freezing – everything you need
to embark upon your first recipe.

Without a little knowledge about the various stages of bread making, you may struggle with the some of terminology that appears in recipes. It may take several months before you can expertly judge the state of your dough, but practice will enable you to become familiar with the concepts, from mixing to the final stage of baking.

PREPARATION

When making bread, it's very important to have everything you need to hand. Timing is vital in the early stages of preparation, because you are working with a live culture. Avoid hunting for ingredients and implements at this crucial point in the preparation process – it will make all the difference between success and failure. The French refer to this stage in baking as *mise en place*, which translates literally as 'setting in place'. You should start by reading the recipe thoroughly and making sure you understand the instructions. Check that your worktops are clean and gather your equipment in one place. Then assemble all the ingredients you require and measure them precisely. Now you are ready to start.

MIXING

The first stage is mixing, when all the ingredients are combined and blended to form a dough.

Begin by putting the flour and salt into a large bowl and mixing them together. Then, using your hand, make a well in the middle. Pour the yeasted water – usually a proportion of the total amount of water in the ingredients – into the well. Again using your hand, start drawing in the flour from the sides of the bowl and mixing it with the liquid until you have a stiff paste.

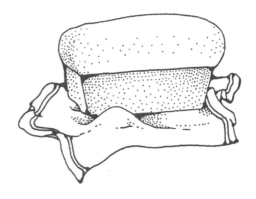

Gradually add the remaining water and continue to mix with your hands, being careful not to make the dough too wet – it should feel damp rather than sticky to the touch. It is important to remember that flour stored in a warm, dry kitchen will absorb more water than flour stored under humid conditions. Check the recipe to see whether the dough should be firm, soft or rough-textured.

KNEADING

This is an essential part of the bread-making process as it stretches the dough and helps the gluten to develop; this gives the bread its final texture. It also encourages the activation of the yeast to give you a light loaf.

Tips before you start

- Dust your hands with flour to prevent the dough from sticking to your skin.
- Wear an apron to cover your clothes – however careful you try to be, you are bound to become covered in flour while you work.
- Always keep some flour handy just in case the dough starts to get too sticky.
- Work at a comfortable height so that you avoid bending over

and straining your back. Use an area with sufficient space to stretch out your arms.

- Make sure your board or work surface is floured before you start (bakers refer to this process as 'bench flouring').

Kneading firm dough Place the dough on the floured surface and fold it in half towards you. Using the heel of your hand (the part between the bottom of the thumb and the wrist), press down and push the dough away from you, while using your other hand to turn it slightly towards you. Continue this folding, pushing and turning motion for the kneading time specified in the recipe. Remember to dust the dough with more flour if it becomes too sticky. After about 10 minutes, the dough will start to change texture, becoming firm, smooth and elastic to the touch. Use the stretch test on page 27 to see if it is ready for proving. If you are happy with the consistency, shape the dough into a ball and place it on a board in a proving bowl. Cover with a clean tea towel and leave to double in size.

Kneading soft dough If your recipe calls for a soft dough, you will need to treat it in a slightly different way to the method described for firm dough. Use a little more bench flour than you would for firm dough, and remove the dough from the bowl with a scraper, as you will find it will stick to your hands. Knead in the same way as suggested for firm dough until the dough loses its stickiness and becomes soft and pliable.

NEED TO KNOW

When you are working with soft dough you may find it constantly sticks to your hands. Dampen them with a little water to get yourself out of this sticky situation.

THE STRETCH TEST

To check whether your dough has been kneaded sufficiently for the gluten to develop its elasticity properly, take a piece and stretch it between your fingers. It should become thin and almost translucent, but it should not tear. If it does tear, continue to knead it for a few more minutes. If it has been overworked – though in fact it is very difficult to overwork dough – it will appear stringy and will tend to stick to your fingers much like a piece of chewed bubblegum.

ADDING OTHER INGREDIENTS

Some of the recipes in this book require the addition of ingredients such as grains, fruit and chopped nuts. These are added later in the mixing stage. Knead the dough for about 5 minutes and then leave it to rest for a further 5 minutes. Press the dough flat into a rough circle and top with the additional ingredients. Fold the dough in half and knead it until the ingredients are evenly distributed. Alternatively, you could use the 'chafing' method described below.

CHAFING

This makes your bread lighter because it expands and lengthens the bubbles of air. It is especially effective for loaves such as focaccia that require an

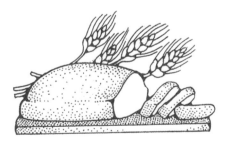

open dough. To chafe, form the dough into a ball and curve your hands round it. Apply a light, downward pressure to the sides, while simultaneously turning the dough continuously in a clockwise motion. Chafing works well if you need to incorporate ingredients such as seeds or nuts (see page 27).

RISING

The speed with which your dough rises will depend on the type of ingredients used and the ambient temperature. For example, dough will rise much faster on a warm humid day than on a cold winter's day. Make allowances for the conditions and choose a suitable place for the dough to rest – in a cool larder on hot days and near a radiator on cold days.

Take care to use a bowl large enough to hold the dough when it has risen. Cover the dough with a clean tea towel and leave it to rise as recommended in the recipe. When your dough has doubled in size and there are air bubbles on the surface (where the carbon dioxide is attempting to escape), it should be ready. Check whether your dough has risen sufficiently by following the guidelines in the box below.

If you have to go out during the rising period, you can slow the process down by placing the dough in the fridge. However, you must bring the dough back

---

NEED TO KNOW

To check that the dough has completed the rising stage, press a finger into the middle of the dough and see what happens:
- if the dough springs back slowly, the dough is ready;
- if the dough springs back immediately it needs a little longer;
- if the dough doesn't spring back at all it is over-risen.

to room temperature before baking, because if you put cold dough straight into a hot oven you will end up with heavy, doughy bread.

KNOCKING BACK

After the dough has risen, you will need to knock the excess gas out of it before the final proving. This process is called 'knocking back' or 'punching down'. If you don't remove the gas, the yeast will continue to ferment and produce gas, and the dough will eventually collapse. Flour your hands and press down into the dough with a clenched fist. You will see it start to deflate.

Scrape the dough from the bowl and turn it out onto a lightly floured work surface. Knead the dough according to the recipe, until it looks as it did before it was left to rise – smooth, soft and elastic.

If you don't want to bake your bread immediately you can leave it to rest for another day as long as you keep knocking it back; this will improve both the flavour and texture of your finished loaf.

SHAPING BASICS

Once the dough has been knocked back, it is time to start shaping it ready for baking. If you are making more than one loaf or want to make rolls, buns etc., you will need to divide the dough into pieces and work it with your hands into the desired shape. Be careful how you handle the dough at this stage – treat it too roughly and the texture will become tight.

When shaping, it is best to work on a wooden board as this keeps the dough warm. If you find the dough is sticking to the surface, lightly dust the board with flour.

Shaping a round Take the dough and gently cup your hands over the top, pressing your fingers lightly into the base. Start to rotate the dough, applying light pressure with your cupped hands to mould it into a round. Continue until you have created a smooth, round shape and the dough is starting to feel tight. If you look at the underside you should see a slight indentation in the middle, which means the dough is ready.

Shaping an oval Create a round shape as above, but cup your hands round the dough and apply gentle pressure until you have an elongated shape.

Shaping a long loaf Press the dough into a flat, round shape. Bring one edge of the dough to the centre, then bring the other edge over the top. Next, seal the folds and press an indentation all the way down the centre. Roll the dough under your palms until you have the desired length.

Shaping rolls Divide the dough into small pieces, just large enough to fit in the palm of your hand. On a floured board, roll each one in a circular motion, lightly pressing out the air, until you have a round shape.

Shaping a cottage loaf Remove one-third of the dough and work this and the larger piece until you have two rounds. Moisten the base of the smaller round with water and place it on top of the larger round. Put the loaf on a greased baking tray and push your index fingers into the centre of the top round and down into the bottom round to seal them together.

Creating a plait Divide your dough into three pieces and roll each one into a long sausage shape, tapered at the ends. With water, moisten one end of each piece and press them together with the heel of your hand. then start to plait them until you have a long loaf. Seal by moistening the other three ends and pressing them together with the heel of your hand. Once you have mastered the art with three pieces you may want to try making a five- or seven-piece plait.

PROVING

Proving is the final stage, when you leave the dough to rise for the last time in a prepared tin or on a baking tray. This is done after you have shaped the dough and it gives you time to preheat the oven ready for baking. As with the first rising stage, the dough should be put in a draught-free, warm place, ideally 24–26°C (75–79°F). Follow the instructions in the recipe and do not leave the dough any longer than recommended or you may find you have a heavy, indigestible loaf. Touching the dough at various stages of proving will give you a guide as to how it is progressing – refer to the box on page 28 for tips on how to recognize when the dough is ready for baking.

If you have allowed the dough to rise too much, knead it gently and leave it to rise again. However, if the dough has collapsed and wrinkles have appeared on the surface there is nothing you can do to save it, since the gluten strands have become overstretched and the loaf will not bake properly.

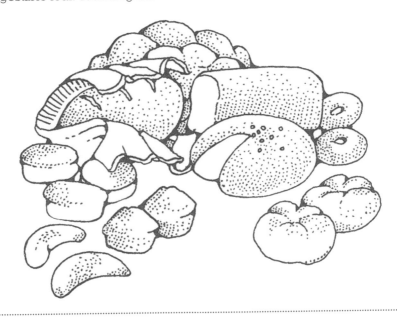

GLAZES AND TOPPINGS

A glaze is usually applied after the final prove and adds colour, flavour and texture to the crust. Possible glazes include egg, honey, maple or golden syrup, milk, milk and egg, olive oil and sugar and water. Apply the glaze to the uncooked dough, using a soft-bristled pastry brush. If you are adding a glaze after the bread is cooked, use a pastry brush and apply it while the bread is still warm.

You can also add toppings before the loaf is cooked by sprinkling them on the glaze. Suggested toppings include chopped nuts, coarse sea salt, fresh herbs, grains, ground or whole spices, rice flour and seeds.

BAKING

At this stage it helps if you are very familiar with your oven, since they do differ. For instance, is yours hotter on one side than the other? If so, you will need to turn the bread halfway through baking. Modern fan ovens seem to avoid this problem because they allow the air to circulate evenly, but you may need to adjust the temperature recommended so as not to burn the crust. Make sure your oven has reached the correct temperature before you start to bake, otherwise your loaf will not rise properly.

Steam This plays an important role in baking many types of bread; not only does it soften the outside of the loaf to assist in the initial rise, it also helps to form a pleasing golden crust.

There are two ways in which you can create a more moist atmosphere in your oven. One way is to spray the sides of your preheated oven with some water as you put the loaf in, repeating the process a couple more times during baking. The other way is to put a roasting tin in the base of the oven with just enough water in it to cover the bottom. Place the tin in the oven a couple of minutes before the bread goes in.

Make sure you follow the recommended baking time carefully and keep an eye on the crust to make sure it isn't burning. Close the door as quickly as possible after placing the bread in the oven, so that you do not lose too much of the heat that has built up inside. The heat of the oven will turn the moisture in the dough into steam, causing the loaf to rise quickly. The heat will deactivate the yeast, allowing the crust to form and go crisp and golden in colour.

The final stages To test whether a loaf is cooked, take it out of the oven using an oven glove, remove it from the tin or baking tray, and tap it on the base. If it is ready it will sound hollow.

As soon as the bread is cooked it should be removed immediately from the oven and the tin and placed on a wire rack to cool. If you leave it in the tin, the steam left inside the loaf will cause it to collapse and it will go gooey, almost like the original uncooked dough.

STORING AND FREEZING

Fresh bread is best eaten on the day it is baked, but you can prolong its life a little by wrapping it in brown paper and keeping it inside a breadbin or crock.

Bread freezes very well. In order to use fuel and time efficiently, make a double batch then, when it is cool, slice up one loaf and store it in a large freezer bag. As a rough guide, one 400g/14oz loaf makes four two-slice sandwiches, several slices of toast or plenty of breadcrumbs to use in other recipes.

TROUBLESHOOTING

With any luck you won't need to use this section, but in case you have a few problems at the beginning, here are a few suggestions to help you avoid or solve most of the common problems you may encounter with your bread.

PROBLEM	CAUSE/SOLUTION
Loaf failed to rise correctly	— Insufficient yeast; make sure you follow the amount given in the recipe — Too much salt added — Underproving, or not allowing enough time for the final prove — Overproving, or allowing too long for final prove; it should only double in size — Temperature was too low where you left the dough to rise — The tins were too large for the amount of dough — The oven temperature was too high
Loaf expanded too much	— The dough was baked before it had finished proving completely — Insufficient salt in the dough – most recipes require 2 per cent of the weight of the flour — The loaf was too large for the tin

PROBLEM	CAUSE/SOLUTION
Loaf spread out but did not rise sufficiently	— Often caused by underkneading the dough — Overproving, or leaving the dough too long in the final rising stage — A wet dough is often prone to this problem, as the gluten structure is delicate and easily deflated
The crust is too dark	— Baking the bread for too long — Oven temperature too high — Too much sugar in the recipe, particularly in enriched breads — If the crust is too dark on the top only, move the shelf further down the oven and slow the process down by placing a sheet of kitchen foil over the loaf — If the bottom of the loaf is getting dark, slide a cold baking tray under the loaf and move the shelf higher in the oven
The crust is too pale	— Oven temperature not high enough — The dough has been allowed to rise in a place that is too warm, making it act as if it were stale, which means the necessary reaction has not taken place and the crust cannot brown — Dough crust dried out during rising; remember to keep it covered

PROBLEM	CAUSE/SOLUTION
The crust is too pale (cont.)	— Lack of water vapour in the oven during the first few minutes of baking; try placing a baking tray with a little water in it in the base of the oven — Some of the enriched breads may have too little sugar
Gap between crust and crumb	— Dough allowed to rise too long in a very dry environment — Final proving period was too short
The crust is too thick	— The final proving stage was too long — The oven temperature was too high — Not enough sugar
White streaks in the crumb	— Usually means that the flour added during the kneading and shaping stages hasn't been mixed in properly. Don't use much – a fine dusting is sufficient to stop the dough from sticking to the surface
Large holes in the crumb	— Usually caused by over-proving of a high-hydration dough — Leaving the dough to prove in too high a temperature. Make sure that the combination of time and temperature is correct

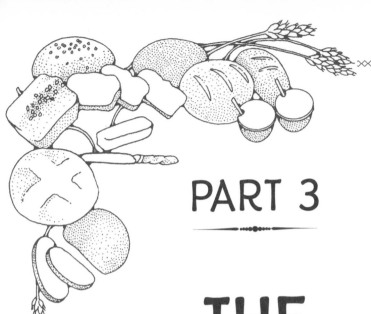

PART 3

THE CLASSICS

The classics are the most readily recognizable recipes and, as the majority are so simple, this is a great place to start. However, don't run before you can walk – learn how to bake the classic white loaf to perfection before moving on to some of the more complicated recipes later in this book.

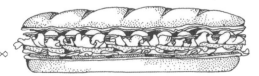

THE CLASSICS

The classics are recipes you will return to again and again,
eventually adding your own personal touches. As you become
accustomed to bread-making techniques you will
gain confidence. But remember, it is best not to move on to a new
recipe until you have mastered the classic white loaf on the
opposite page and it turns out perfectly every time.

Most of the recipes in this book use easy-blend dried yeast which comes in handy 7g/¼oz sachets (the correct amount for 450g/1lb flour) or in tubs. If you wish to use fresh yeast, allow 14g/½oz (double the quantity of dried) and mix it with some of the warm liquid before adding it to the flour mixture. Leave it at room temperature until a froth forms on the surface.

Read all the instructions thoroughly before you start, to make sure you understand them completely. Work methodically through each stage until you become accustomed to the sequence of mix, rise, knock back, shape, prove and bake. After a while, the process will become second nature to you.

If you are using a fan-assisted oven, reduce the temperature by 20° and the cooking time by 5–10 minutes as fan ovens tend to cook food faster than conventional ovens.

NEED TO KNOW

Whether your yeast is fresh or dried, always check the 'use by' date, as stale yeast won't activate properly.

CLASSIC WHITE LOAF

This is a traditional recipe for a white loaf, but made with milk instead of water to produce a softer crumb.

INGREDIENTS *Makes 1 loaf*

450g/1lb strong white bread flour

2 tsp fine salt

1 tsp caster sugar

1 sachet easy-blend yeast

60g/2oz unsalted butter, room temperature and diced

300ml/10fl oz whole milk at 37°C/98.6°F

METHOD

1. Put the flour, salt, sugar and yeast in a large bowl and mix thoroughly. Add the diced butter and work with your fingers until the mixture resembles fine breadcrumbs.

2. Make a well in the centre, add the milk a little at a time and mix with your hands until you have a smooth and elastic dough.

3. Turn the dough out onto a lightly floured surface and knead for 5 minutes or until it is smooth.

4. Place the dough in a lightly oiled bowl, cover with a damp tea towel and leave to rise in a warm place for 1 hour, or until it has doubled in size.

5. Preheat the oven to 200°C/ 400°F/gas mark 6. Grease a 900g/2lb loaf tin with butter.

6. Knock back the dough and turn it out onto a lightly floured surface. Knead the dough for 5 minutes, then shape it into a rough circle and place it in the prepared tin. Cover with the tea towel and leave to prove for 10 minutes or until doubled in size.

7. Dust the the loaf with flour. Place in the oven and bake for 30–35 minutes or until golden brown. Turn out of the tin and leave to cool on a wire rack before slicing.

WHOLEMEAL LOAF

This classic wholemeal loaf is made from flour milled using 100 per cent of the grain. It is a looser texture than the classic white, so don't be surprised if it crumbles a little when slicing.

INGREDIENTS *Makes 1 large loaf*
450g/1lb strong wholemeal
   bread flour
1 tsp fine salt
1 tsp granulated sugar
1 sachet easy-blend yeast
15g/½oz unsalted butter, room
   temperature and diced
300ml/10fl oz hand-hot water
1 tbsp porridge oats

METHOD

1. Mix the flour, salt, sugar and yeast in a large bowl. Add the diced butter and work it with your fingertips until the mixture resembles fine breadcrumbs.

2. Make a well in the centre of the flour mixture and gradually add the water, bringing in the flour from the sides of the bowl. Mix together with your hands until a soft dough starts to form.

3. Turn the dough out onto a lightly floured surface and knead until it is smooth and elastic in texture – about 10 minutes.

4. Place the dough in a large, lightly oiled bowl and cover with a damp tea towel. Leave in a warm place, ideally a warm kitchen or airing cupboard, to rise until it is double in size. This should take approximately 1 hour.

5. Preheat the oven to 230°C/450°F/gas mark 8 and grease a 900g/2lb loaf tin with butter.

6. Once the dough has risen, turn it out onto a lightly floured surface and knock back to remove the air. Knead for a further 5–10 minutes.

7. Shape the dough into a rough oval shape and put into the prepared tin. Cover with a damp tea towel and leave to rise in a warm place until it has doubled in size; the bread should have risen to the top of the tin (approximately 30–35 minutes).

8. When the dough has finished proving, dust the top of the loaf with some wholemeal flour and a few porridge oats to give it a rustic coating.

9. Place the loaf in the centre of the preheated oven and bake for 15 minutes. Reduce the oven temperature to 200°C/400°F/gas mark 6 and bake for a further 15–20 minutes or until the bread has risen and the crust is golden brown. The loaf is ready if it sounds hollow when tapped on the base.

NEED TO KNOW

To make a light wholemeal loaf that rises exceptionally high, use the butter cold from the fridge rather than at room temperature and add it little by little after the first kneading stage. Knead each sliver of butter into the dough until it is thoroughly blended. This has the effect of 'greasing' the strands of gluten instead of the butter being absorbed into the flour.

GRANARY LOAF

This granary loaf has a distinctive malty, almost nutty flavour which works well as a ploughman's lunch or with a bowl of steaming soup. Alternatively, it's delicious served with cream and jam.

INGREDIENTS *Makes 1 large loaf*
500g/1lb 2 oz granary bread flour
1¼ tsp fine salt
1 tsp caster sugar
30g/1oz butter at room
    temperature, diced
1½ tsp dried yeast
300ml/10fl oz warm water

METHOD

1. In a large bowl, mix together the flour, salt and sugar. Add the diced butter and rub into the flour with your fingertips, lifting the dry ingredients to allow air into the mixture. The finished mixture should resemble fine breadcrumbs.

2. Add the yeast and mix thoroughly, then make a well in the centre of the flour mixture.

3. Gradually add the warm water and mix with your hands until a soft dough has formed.

4. Turn the dough out onto a floured surface and knead for 10–15 minutes or until the dough has a soft and elastic texture.

5. Place a large glass bowl in warm water for a few minutes, then dry and oil lightly. Place the dough in the warm bowl and cover with a damp tea towel. Leave the dough to rise for approximately 2 hours or until it has doubled in size.

6. Once it has risen sufficiently, knock back the dough and turn it out onto a lightly floured surface. Knead for a further 10–15 minutes.

7. Grease a 900g/2lb loaf tin with butter. Shape the dough into a rough oval and ease it into the prepared tin. Cover the tin with a damp tea towel and leave the dough to prove for about 1 hour; it should double in size and reach the top of the tin.

8. Towards the end of the proving time, preheat your oven to 160°C/325°F/gas mark 3.

9. Once the dough has risen sufficiently, bake in the centre of the preheated oven for 15 minutes. Increase the oven temperature to 200°C/400°F/gas mark 6 and continue to bake until the loaf has risen and is golden brown on the top.

10. Remove the loaf from the oven, turn it out of the tin and leave to cool on a wire rack.

For a soft crust

Dust the top with flour before baking and wrap the loaf in a clean, dry tea towel while it is cooling on the wire rack.

For a crisp, golden crust

Brush the top of the loaf with beaten egg before baking.

VARIATION

If you would like to make rolls instead of a single loaf, divide the dough into 12 pieces after the second kneading stage. Form these into rounds using your hands and place them on a large, greased baking tray, leaving plenty of room between each one. Cover the rolls with a damp tea towel and leave to rise until they have doubled in size.

Bake in a preheated oven at 200°C/400°F/gas mark 6 and reduce the cooking time to 10–15 minutes.

SOFT WHITE DINNER ROLLS

Homemade dinner rolls taste far better than any shop bought ones. With their mild, slightly buttery flavour they are a wonderful addition to your bread basket.

INGREDIENTS *Makes 16 rolls*
450g/1lb strong white bread flour
1¼ tsp fine salt
40g/1¼ oz caster sugar
1 sachet easy-blend yeast
20g/¾oz skimmed milk powder
40g/1¼oz instant mashed potato granules
85g/3oz unsalted butter at room temperature, diced
240–270ml/8–9fl oz lukewarm water

METHOD

1. Combine all the dry ingredients in a large bowl. Add the diced butter and work it into the dry ingredients with your fingertips until the mixture resembles breadcrumbs. Make a well in the centre.

2. Gradually add the lukewarm water and work the mixture together with your hands until a soft dough is formed. Turn it out onto a lightly floured surface and knead for 10 minutes or until the dough has a soft and elastic texture.

3. Lightly grease a bowl and place the dough in it. Cover with a damp tea towel and leave in a warm place for about 1 hour or until it has doubled in size.

4. Grease two baking trays with butter. After the dough has risen sufficiently, knock back and turn it out onto a lightly floured surface. Divide the dough into 16 pieces and shape each piece by rolling it under the palm of your hand until it forms a smooth ball.

5. Place 8 rolls on each baking

tray, allowing plenty of space between each one. Cover the trays with damp tea towels or lightly greased cling film. Leave them in a warm place for about 1 hour, or until they are puffy and double in size.

6. Preheat your oven to 180°C/350°F/gas mark 4.

7. When you are happy that the rolls have risen sufficiently, place the baking trays in the centre of the preheated oven and cook for 20–25 minutes, or until the rolls are golden brown on top and a little lighter on the sides.

8. Remove the rolls from the oven and after a couple of minutes carefully transfer them to a wire rack to cool.

TIPS

If you want a soft, buttery crust, brush the tops of the rolls with melted butter as soon as they come out of the oven.

If you want floury rolls, gently sift flour onto the surface after you remove them from the oven.

For seedy toppings, brush the tops of the rolls with milk before baking and sprinkle with sesame seeds, poppy seeds or any other seed of choice.

CLASSIC FRENCH STICK

A traditional French stick or baguette is very crusty and light because it is cooked at an extremely high temperature in a moist atmosphere. To achieve the correct texture this recipe uses a simple starter which will need to be made in advance.

INGREDIENTS *Makes 3 baguettes*

FOR THE STARTER:

120ml/4fl oz cool water

¼ tsp dried yeast

125g/4½oz strong white
   bread flour

FOR THE BREAD:

1 tsp dried yeast

230–300ml/7½–10fl oz lukewarm
   water

450g/1lb strong white bread flour

1½ tsp fine sea salt

2 tbsp polenta

METHOD

1. The day before baking, make the starter by mixing the cool water and yeast in a glass bowl. Add the flour, cover and leave at room temperature for 12–15 hours. When the starter has risen and has bubbles on the surface, it is ready.

2. To make the dough, mix the yeast with the lukewarm water in a large bowl. Add the flour, the starter and the salt and mix together with your hands until you have a soft dough.

3. Turn the dough out onto a lightly floured surface and knead for 5–10 minutes or until it is smooth and elastic in texture.

4. Lightly oil a large bowl, place the dough in it and cover with a damp tea towel. Leave to rise in a warm place for 1 hour.

5. Knock back the dough, turn it over, cover the bowl again and leave to rise for a further hour.

6. Repeat step 5 so the

dough has been left to rise for a total of 3 hours.

7. Lightly grease your work surface to prevent the dough from sticking and turn it out from the bowl. Divide the dough into three equal portions. Cover and leave to rest for 15 minutes.

8. Take each piece of dough, fold it in half lengthways and seal the edges with the heel of your hand. Repeat this step.

9. With the seam side down, gently roll the dough with your hands until you have 3 long, slim baguettes.

10. Line a large baking tray with parchment that has been sprinkled with polenta and place the baguettes seam-side down. Cover with a damp tea towel or oiled cling film and leave to prove for a further 90 minutes.

11. Towards the end of the final proving time, preheat your oven to 230°C/450°F/gas mark 8.

12. Using a sharp knife, make three cuts at an angle in the top

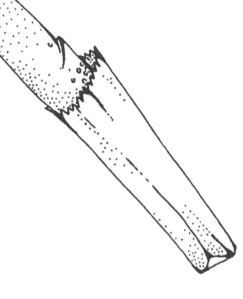

of each baguette. For a nice crisp crust, sprinkle them liberally with warm water.

13. Bake the baguettes in the centre of the oven for 25–30 minutes or until they are golden brown.

14. Remove the baguettes from the oven and leave to cool on a wire rack. These are best eaten warm, on the day of baking.

COTTAGE LOAF

———— •••◦❂◦••• ————

This classic British recipe has all the rustic charm of a farmhouse kitchen. It is characterized by its shape, that of two round loaves, one nestling on top of the other.

INGREDIENTS *Makes 1 large loaf*
1½ tsp dried yeast
300ml/10fl oz warm milk
450g/1lb strong white bread flour
1 tsp fine salt
1 beaten egg, to glaze

METHOD

1. Sprinkle the yeast into the milk in a glass bowl and leave in a warm place for 15 minutes until a froth has formed on the surface.
2. Put the flour and salt into a large mixing bowl and make a well in the centre. Pour in the yeast liquid and mix together with your hands until the dough leaves the sides of the bowl clean.
3. Turn the dough out onto a lightly floured surface and knead for 10 minutes until it has a smooth and elastic texture.
4. Place the dough in a lightly greased bowl, cover with a damp tea towel and leave to rise for 1 hour or until it has doubled in size.
5. Once the dough has risen, knock back, turn out onto a floured surface and knead very lightly for 3–4 minutes.
6. Cut off one-third of the dough and shape into a round. Dust your hands and the dough with

flour, then rub your hands over the surface of the dough to give it an even covering. Pick up the dough with both hands, making sure your thumbs are on top and your fingers underneath. Working quickly, use your thumbs andthe palms of your hands to gently stretch the dough downwards, at the same time tucking the excess dough underneath with your fingers. Rotate the dough a quarter turn and repeat the above until you have an evenly shaped ball with a smooth surface.

7. Follow the same procedure with the remaining piece of dough, this time making a much larger round.

8. Grease a baking tray with butter and place the larger round on it. Brush the top of the large round with a little water, then place the smaller round on top.

9. Using your index fingers, push down through the centre of the smaller round right into the lower round, making a hole in the middle.

10. Using a sharp knife, make cuts at 5cm/2in intervals around the top round. Cover the loaf with a damp tea towel and leave in a warm place for about 30 minutes or until the dough has doubled in size.

11. Preheat the oven to 230°C/450°F/gas mark 8. Using a pastry brush, glaze the surface of the loaf with a little beaten egg.

12. Bake the loaf in the centre of the oven for 10 minutes, then reduce the temperature to 200°C/400°F/gas mark 6. Bake for a further 20–25 minutes or until the crust is golden brown. When it is ready, the cottage loaf should sound hollow when tapped on the base.

13. Remove the loaf from the oven and transfer it to a wire rack to cool.

SOURDOUGH BREAD

This classic bread is believed to date back to Ancient Egypt, some 5,000 years ago, and derives its characteristic 'tang' from a fermented starter that is used to enhance the flavour.

INGREDIENTS *Makes 1 large loaf*
500g/1lb 2 oz strong white
    bread flour
1 tsp fine salt
200g/7oz sourdough starter (see
    page 15)
250ml/8fl oz lukewarm water

METHOD
1. Mix the flour with the salt in a large bowl and make a well in the centre. Weigh the amount of sourdough starter required and mix it with the lukewarm water. Pour it into the well in the flour and gradually work the flour into the liquid to form a soft dough.
2. Turn the dough out onto a floured surface and knead for 10 minutes or until it is soft and pliable.

NEED TO KNOW

The rising time of the dough depends on the room temperature and the strength of your starter. If your starter is new, the dough will take longer to rise than if the starter is well established.

Lightly oil a clean bowl and place the dough in it. Cover the bowl with a damp tea towel and leave the dough to rise in a warm place for 3–4 hours or until it has doubled in size.

3. Knock back the dough to its original size and then turn it onto a floured work surface. Shape the dough into a ball and place in a colander lined with a floured tea towel. Cover with a damp tea towel and leave for 2–4 hours or until doubled in size.

4. When your dough is nearly ready, preheat the oven to 220°C/425°F/gas mark 7 and place a bowl containing some water on the base of the oven to produce extra moisture.

5. Invert the dough onto a greased baking tray and make three diagonal cuts in the surface. Bake in the centre of the oven for about 35 minutes.

6. Transfer the bread to a wire rack to cool before eating. Although best eaten fresh, sourdough makes wonderful, slightly chewy toast.

USING OLD DOUGH

A long-established way of leavening bread is to use a piece of old dough. Simply remove a portion of the dough after the first rising period and keep it, covered, in the refrigerator for 2 days.

When you are ready to use the dough as a starter for a new loaf, take it out of the refrigerator and leave it to rest at room temperature for about 3 hours.

Alternatively, you can freeze the dough for up to 6 months. First wrap it in a piece of greaseproof paper and then in a layer of kitchen foil. To thaw, leave it overnight in the refrigerator before letting it stand at room temperature for 3 hours.

MILK LOAF

As with the sourdough bread, this recipe for a milk loaf also uses a starter – but this time it's a sponge. Because the milk is scalded before being added to the recipe, the crumb of this loaf is particularly light and fluffy.

INGREDIENTS *Makes 1 large loaf*

FOR THE SPONGE STARTER:

230ml/7½fl oz full cream milk

60ml (2fl oz) double cream

1 sachet easy-blend yeast

175g/6oz strong white
    bread flour

FOR THE DOUGH:

1 tbsp golden syrup

200g/7oz strong white
    bread flour

1 tsp fine salt

30g/1oz unsalted butter, melted

1 egg, beaten

METHOD

1. Start by making your sponge starter. Place the milk and cream in a saucepan and bring to the boil. Remove from the heat, pour into a jug and leave until lukewarm. Don't worry if a skin forms on the surface – this won't affect the starter. Top up the liquid with some warm water until you have 250ml/8fl oz.

2. Pour the liquid into a large bowl and add the yeast and flour. Stir with a wooden spoon until the mixture forms a smooth batter. Cover the bowl and leave for 2–4 hours in a warm place. The mixture is ready when it has frothed up and collapsed a little in the middle.

3. When your sponge has fermented, add the golden syrup and beat with a wooden spoon.

4. Add the second batch of flour, the salt and melted butter. Mix until you have a sticky dough.

5. Over a period of 30 minutes, give the dough three light kneads of about 2–3 minutes each. Don't be heavy-handed with the dough at this stage otherwise you will end up with a stodgy crumb after it is baked. After the three kneads, cover the dough with a damp tea towel and leave in a warm place for 30 minutes.

6. Lightly flour your work surface and the surface of a rolling pin. Gently roll the dough out into a rectangle and then roll it up tightly to form a cylindrical shape.

7. Grease a 900g/2lb loaf tin and dust it with flour to stop the loaf sticking. Place the dough seam-side down in the tin, cover it with a damp tea towel and leave in a warm place for about 1½ hours or until it has doubled in size.

8. Towards the end of the rising time, preheat the oven to 220°C/ 425°F/gas mark 7 and place a bowl of water in the base of the oven to create moisture.

9. Brush the top of the loaf with beaten egg and score with a sharp knife at regular intervals.

10. Bake in the centre of the preheated oven for 20 minutes, then reduce the temperature to 200°C/400°F/gas mark 6. Bake for a further 20–25 minutes until the crust is a golden brown.

11. Remove the loaf from the oven, turn it out of the tin and leave to cool on a wire rack.

RUSTIC RYE BREAD

Rye flour is highly nutritious and makes a darker, denser loaf than wheat. It can be used alone or mixed with white or wholemeal wheat flour to produce a less coarse crumb.

Makes 1 large loaf
3½ tsp dried yeast
300ml/10fl oz lukewarm water
400g/14oz strong white
    bread flour
110g/4oz rye flour
1½ tsp fine salt
60g/2oz unsalted butter, at room
    temperature, diced

METHOD

1. Sprinkle the yeast into the water in a glass bowl and leave in a warm place for 15 minutes or until a froth has formed.

2. Place the flours and salt in a large mixing bowl. Add the diced butter and work the mixture until it resembles breadcrumbs. Make a well in the centre.

3. Gradually add the yeast mixture to the flour and work it in, bringing the flour in from the sides until you have a soft dough.

4. Turn the dough out onto a lightly floured surface and knead for 5 minutes until it has a smooth, elastic texture. Place it in a lightly oiled bowl, cover with a damp tea towel and leave to rise for 1 hour, or until double in size.

5. Knock back, then tip the dough out onto a lightly floured surface and knead for about 3 minutes. Shape into a ball,then slightly flatten and dust the top with flour. Using a sharp knife, mark a cross on the surface. Place the dough on a greased baking tray, cover with a damp tea towel and leave to prove for a further hour, or until it has doubled in size.

6. Preheat your oven to 220°C/425°F/gas mark 7.

7. Place the loaf in the centre of the oven and bake for 25–30 minutes, or until the crust is golden brown. Remove from the tray and leave to cool on a wire rack.

RYE BREADSTICKS

INGREDIENTS *Makes 24 sticks*
20g/¾oz dried yeast
315ml/10½fl oz warm water
500g/1lb 2oz rye flour
500g/1lb 2 oz strong white
    bread flour
3 tbsp sugar
1 tsp salt
30g/1oz butter, at room
    temperature, diced
1 tbsp caraway seeds
30g/1oz butter, melted

METHOD
1. Sprinkle the yeast into 120ml/4fl oz warm water in a glass bowl and stir until dissolved.
2. Put the two flours, sugar and salt in another bowl and mix until combined. Add the diced butter and work the mixture with your fingers until it resembles breadcrumbs. Make a well in the centre, add the yeast mixture and slowly add the remainder of the water until a soft dough forms.
3. Follow the recipe for Rustic Rye Bread (facing page) until shaping the dough. Cut the dough in half and then cut each half into 12 equal pieces. Roll each piece until it is about 15cm/6in long. Place them about 5cm/2in apart on greased baking trays. Cover and leave to rise for 30 minutes. Brush with melted butter and sprinkle with caraway seeds.
4. Preheat the oven to 200°C/400°F/gas mark 6. Bake the breadsticks in the centre of the oven for 15–20 minutes or until golden brown. Cool on a wire rack before serving.

MIXED SEED LOAF

This is a delicious alternative to a plain white loaf; the addition of seeds and buttermilk gives the bread a uniquely rich and buttery flavour.

INGREDIENTS *Makes 2 loaves*
1 sachet easy-blend yeast
175g/6oz caster sugar
175ml/6fl oz warm water
360ml/12fl oz buttermilk, at room
  temperature
40g/1¼oz butter, melted
3 tbsp runny honey
1½ tsp fine salt
30g/1oz sesame seeds
30g/1oz flax seeds
30g/1oz poppy seeds
30g/1oz sunflower seeds
250g/9oz wholemeal bread flour
550g/1¼lb strong white
  bread flour

METHOD
1. Dissolve the yeast and sugar in the warm water and leave to stand for about 10 minutes until the mixture is creamy and slightly frothy.
2. In a large bowl, mix together the buttermilk, butter, honey and yeast mixture. Add the salt, all of the seeds and the wholemeal flour. Stir thoroughly with a wooden spoon to combine.
3. Add the white flour a little at a time, mixing well with the wooden spoon after each addition. Once you have

incorporated all the flour, mix with your hands until you have a smooth dough.

4. Turn the dough out onto a lightly floured board and knead for 5–6 minutes or until it is smooth and elastic in texture.

5. Lightly oil a large bowl, place the dough inside and turn to coat it with the oil. Cover with a damp tea towel and leave in a warm place for about 1 hour, or until it has doubled in size.

6. Preheat the oven to 190°C/ 375°F/gas mark 5. Grease two 23cm × 12cm/9in × 5in loaf tins with butter.

7. Knock back the dough and turn it out onto a lightly floured surface. Divide it in half and form each half into a rectangle. Place the dough in the prepared tins. Cover with a damp tea towel and leave to rise until doubled in size, which should take about 40 minutes.

8. Place the loaves in the centre of the preheated oven and bake for about 30 minutes or until the crust is golden brown. The loaves

---

NEED TO KNOW

If you have any problems obtaining buttermilk, don't let that put you off trying this recipe as you can make buttermilk easily at home.

Real buttermilk is the slightly sour liquid that is left over after the production of butter. Using vinegar to curdle milk produces much the same result. Simply place 250ml (8fl oz) milk in a bowl, add 1 tablespoon of white vinegar and leave the mixture for 5 minutes. If your recipe requires more, just increase the ingredients proportionally.

---

should sound hollow when tapped on the base.

9. Turn the loaves out of the tins and leave to cool on a wire rack before slicing.

IRISH SODA BREAD

This traditional soda bread has a nutty flavour resulting from the combination of wholemeal and white flour and is really quick to make, as it uses a chemical raising agent instead of yeast.

INGREDIENTS *Makes 1 large loaf*
250g/9oz plain white flour
250g/9oz wholemeal flour
1 tsp bicarbonate of soda
½ tsp salt
300ml/10fl oz buttermilk

METHOD
1. Preheat the oven to 200°C/400°F/gas mark 6.
2. Mix the white and wholemeal flours, bicarbonate of soda and salt in a large bowl.
3. Make a well in the centre of the flour mixture and gradually pour in the buttermilk. Pull the flour in from the edges of the bowl and work until you have a soft dough.
4. Turn the dough out onto a floured surface and knead lightly for a couple of minutes or until it forms a smooth ball.

5. Place the dough on a greased baking tray and flatten slightly so that it forms a domed, round loaf. Using a sharp knife, cut a cross in the top of the loaf. Sprinkle with a little wholemeal flour.
6. Place the loaf in the centre of the oven and bake for 30 minutes or until it is well risen and the crust is brown. When it is ready the loaf will sound hollow when tapped on the base.
7. Transfer the loaf to a wire rack and leave it to cool completely before slicing.

Soda bread goes stale very quickly, so should be eaten on the day of baking. It makes very good toast, so if you have any left you can enjoy it for breakfast the following day.

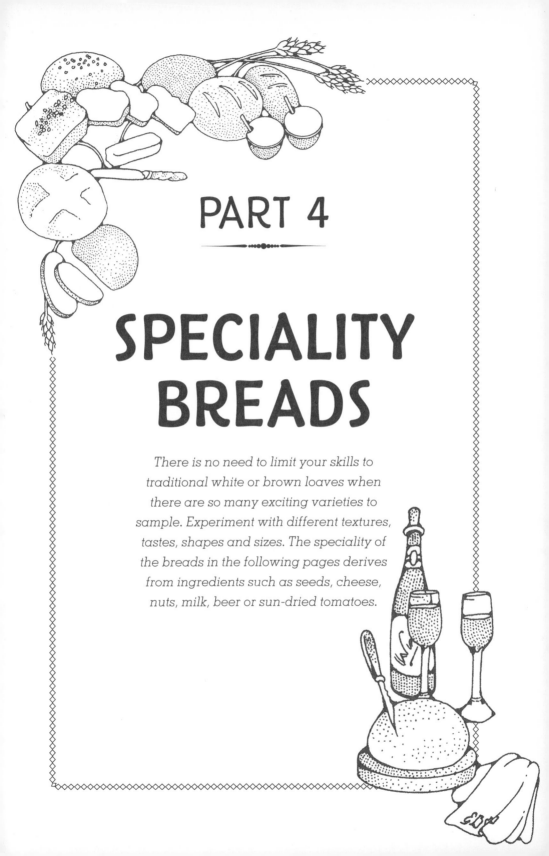

PART 4

SPECIALITY BREADS

There is no need to limit your skills to
traditional white or brown loaves when
there are so many exciting varieties to
sample. Experiment with different textures,
tastes, shapes and sizes. The speciality of
the breads in the following pages derives
from ingredients such as seeds, cheese,
nuts, milk, beer or sun-dried tomatoes.

GAINING CONFIDENCE

Once you are having more successes than failures with the classics it's time to move on to the next stage of baking – experimenting with flavours and textures.

As you explore your new hobby you will find many exciting ingredients can be included in your recipes. This procedure is no more complicated than, say, adding an extra ingredient to your favourite sauce or putting dates instead of raisins in a bread and butter pudding. You will soon instinctively know which flavours will complement one another in your breads.

This section of the book aims to give you some ideas for ingredients and accustom you to using different combinations. The same basics that apply to classic loaves also hold true for speciality breads so you won't have any new techniques to learn, except for experimenting with a few different shapes.

You will have gained a lot of experience baking the classic loaves, learning when to add more flour or water and how long to knead the dough to get exactly the right measure of elasticity. This means you can now move on with confidence to some more unusual recipes.

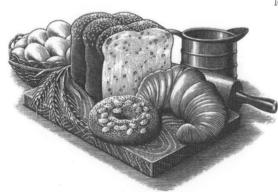

OLIVE & ROSEMARY BREAD

This delicious bread flavoured with olives and fragrant rosemary is very easy to make and wonderful served warm with cheese.

INGREDIENTS *Makes 1 loaf*
450g/1lb strong white
   bread flour
1 sachet easy-blend yeast
1½ tsp sea salt
1 tbsp golden caster sugar
175g/6oz pitted green olives,
   sliced
3 tbsp extra virgin olive oil
240–300ml/8–10fl oz warm water
6 sprigs rosemary

METHOD

1. Put the flour, yeast, salt, sugar and olives in a large bowl. Add the olive oil and enough warm water to make a dough. Mix all the ingredients with your hands.
2. Turn the dough out onto a lightly floured surface and knead for 10 minutes until it is smooth and elastic in texture.
3. Put the dough in a greased bowl, cover with a damp tea towel and leave in a warm place for 30 minutes or until it has doubled in size.
4. Knock back the dough and knead for 2–3 minutes, then place it in a greased 25cm/10in loaf tin. Remove the leaves from the rosemary sprigs and press into the surface of the loaf. Cover with a damp tea towel and leave to rise in a warm place until the dough has doubled in size. This should take around 30 minutes.
5. While the dough is proving, preheat the oven to 220°C/425°F/gas mark 7.
6. Place the loaf in the centre of the oven, reduce the oven temperature to 200°C/400°F/gas mark 6 and bake for 35 minutes or until the loaf is golden brown. Turn it out of the tin, tap the base to check that it sounds hollow, then cool on a wire rack.

DATE & WALNUT ROLLS

These rolls make an excellent breakfast served warm with slices of banana, apple, peach or any other fruit that is in season.

Makes 9 rolls
375g/13oz strong white
  bread flour
25g/1oz brown sugar
1 sachet easy-blend yeast
1 tsp salt
250ml/8fl oz warm milk
50g/1¾oz butter
1 egg
115g/4oz chopped dates
115g/4oz chopped walnuts
1 tsp vanilla essence

1. In a large mixing bowl, combine the flour, sugar, yeast and salt.
2. Put the milk and butter in a saucepan and heat over a medium heat until the butter has completely melted.
3. Add the warm liquid, egg, dates, walnuts and vanilla to the dry ingredients in the bowl. Mix with your hands until the dough is easy to handle. If it is too sticky, add a little more flour.
4. Turn the dough out onto a floured surface and knead for 5 minutes or until it is smooth and elastic. Form the dough into a ball and place in a greased bowl. Cover with a damp tea towel and leave in a warm place for about 1 hour – it should double in size.
5. Knock back the dough, divide into 9 portions and shape into individual rolls. Place the rolls on a greased baking tray, leaving plenty of room between each one. Cover with a tea towel and leave to rise for 30 minutes.
6. Preheat the oven to 180°C/350°F/gas mark 4. Uncover the rolls and bake in the centre of the oven for 15–20 minutes or until golden brown. Remove from the oven and cool on a wire rack.

CORNBREAD

This is a traditional bread from the American South that should be eaten warm, straight from the oven, to appreciate its fresh flavour.

INGREDIENTS *Serves 4–6*
300g/10oz cornmeal
85g/3oz plain flour
2 tsp bicarbonate of soda
salt and freshly ground
    black pepper
1 egg
150ml/5fl oz milk
420ml/14½fl oz buttermilk
1 mild red chilli, deseeded and
    finely chopped
200g/7oz can sweetcorn

METHOD

1. Preheat the oven to 200°C/400°F/gas mark 6. Grease a shallow 25-cm-/10-in-long roasting tin with butter.
2. Combine the cornmeal, flour and bicarbonate of soda in a large bowl and season well with salt and pepper. Form a well in the centre.
3. Mix together the egg, milk, buttermilk, chillies and sweetcorn and pour into the well in the centre of the dry ingredients. Mix gently until the ingredients are thoroughly combined, but do not overwork it at this stage otherwise the cornbread will be doughy and tough when cooked.
4. Pour the mixture into the greased tin and bake in the preheated oven for 25–30 minutes or until it is firm and golden.
5. Cut the cornbread into squares and serve warm.

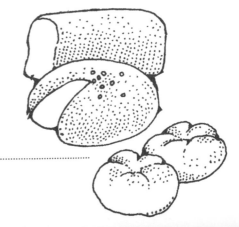

RYE & CRÈME FRAÎCHE BREAD

Sliced thinly and buttered, this bread makes a wonderful accompaniment to smoked salmon and a green salad.

INGREDIENTS *Makes 1 large loaf*
175g/6oz rye flour
175g/6oz wholemeal flour
115g/4oz strong white bread flour
2 tbsp finely chopped fresh dill
zest of 1 lemon, finely grated
2 tsp fine salt
25g/scant 1oz dark brown sugar
1 tsp dried yeast
250ml/8fl oz warm water
150ml/5fl oz crème fraîche

METHOD

1. Mix the three flours in a large bowl and then stir in the dill, lemon zest, salt and sugar.
2. Dissolve the yeast in 1 tablespoon of the warm water and leave to stand for 5 minutes.
3. Make a well in the centre of the flour mixture and pour in the yeast, the crème fraîche and enough of the remaining water to form a smooth, soft dough.

4. Turn the dough out onto a lightly floured surface and knead for 5 minutes until it is smooth and elastic in texture. Place it in a lightly oiled bowl, cover with a damp tea towel and leave to rise for 1 hour, until doubled in size.
5. Knock back the dough and turn out onto a floured surface. Knead for a further 5 minutes and then shape into a round loaf. Place the loaf on a greased baking tray and make three diagonal cuts in the top with a sharp knife. Cover with a damp tea towel and leave to prove for 30 minutes.
6. Preheat the oven to 200°C/400°F/ gas mark 6.
7. Place the loaf in the oven and bake for 25–30 minutes. It should be browned and sound hollow when tapped on the base.
8. Remove from the tray. Leave to cool on a wire rack before slicing.

PUMPERNICKEL

Pumpernickel bread originated in Germany in the 15th century and is characterized by its dark colour and nutty rye taste.

Makes 2 loaves
360ml/12fl oz warm water
2 tbsp caster sugar
2 tsp dried yeast
½ tsp salt
2 eggs, beaten
75g/2½oz molasses
60ml/2fl oz vegetable oil
300g/10oz strong white bread flour
140g/5oz wholewheat flour
140g/5oz rye flour
1 tsp instant coffee
2 tbsp cocoa powder
1 egg, beaten, for glazing

1. Put the water in a large mixing bowl and add the sugar, yeast and salt. Leave for 5 minutes. When you see bubbles starting to form on the surface, add the eggs, molasses and oil. Combine the flours, coffee and cocoa powder and gradually add to the bowl. Mix in well with your hands, making sure all the ingredients are incorporated.

2. Turn the dough out onto a lightly floured board and knead for 10 minutes until it is smooth but slightly sticky. Place it in a warm, lightly oiled bowl, cover with a damp tea towel and leave for 2 hours or until doubled in size.

3. Knock back and then knead lightly for 2–3 minutes. Divide the dough into 2 equal portions and shape into rounds or ovals. Place the loaves on greased baking trays and brush the surface of each loaf with beaten egg. Cover with a damp tea towel and leave to rise for a further hour.

4. Preheat the oven to 190°C/375°F/gas mark 5 and bake the loaves for 25 minutes or until dark in colour. Leave to cool on a wire rack before serving.

PARMESAN & COURGETTE BREAD

This is a surprising flavour combination which works extremely well, especially when teamed with cheese or cured meat.

INGREDIENTS *Makes 1 large loaf*
500g/1lb 2oz strong white bread
    flour
1½ tsp fine salt
1 tsp garlic powder
1 sachet easy-blend yeast
2 tbsp light olive oil
250ml/8fl oz warm water
4 medium courgettes, grated
6 tbsp grated Parmesan cheese
extra virgin olive oil
coarse sea salt

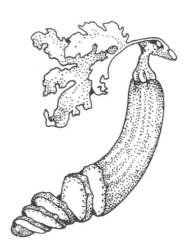

METHOD
1. Put the flour, salt, garlic powder and yeast in a large bowl. Make a well in the centre and add the olive oil and enough warm water to form a soft dough. Mix until the dough comes away from the sides of the bowl.
2. Turn the dough out onto a lightly floured surface and knead for 5 minutes until it is smooth

NEED TO KNOW

If you are making cuts in the top of your loaf it helps to put a little oil on the blade to prevent it from dragging across the soft dough.

and elastic in texture. Place it in
a lightly oiled bowl and leave
to rise for 1 hour or until it has
doubled in size.

3. While the dough is rising, grate
the courgettes onto a clean tea
towel and then squeeze out all
the excess water. Put in a bowl
with the grated Parmesan and
mix together.

4. Knock back the dough, turn
out onto a lightly floured surface
and add the grated courgette
and Parmesan. Knead the
dough until the ingredients are
thoroughly mixed.

5. Shape the dough into an oval.
Brush the top lightly with olive
oil and sprinkle with coarse sea
salt. Cover the loaf with a damp
tea towel and leave to prove
for another hour or until it has
doubled in size.

6. Preheat the oven to 200°C/
400°F/gas mark 6.

7. Bake the loaf in the preheated
oven for 20–30 minutes or until it
is golden and the base sounds
hollow when tapped.

8. Drizzle with a little more olive
oil while the loaf is still warm

and leave to cool on a wire rack
before serving.

VARIATION

Instead of using Parmesan
cheese, try roasting 2
garlic bulbs in the oven at
200°C/400°F/gas mark 6 for
20 minutes. Leave to cool
then squeeze the garlic out
of each individual clove. Mix
the garlic with the grated
courgette and continue
from Step 4, omitting the
Parmesan cheese.

BEER BREAD WITH HONEY

You can use any type of beer to make this bread, but brown ale gives it a rich flavour and a lovely dark colour.

INGREDIENTS *Makes 1 large loaf*
300ml/10fl oz brown ale
60g/2oz unsalted butter, softened
1 tbsp runny honey
225g/8oz strong white bread flour
225g/8oz wholemeal flour
1 tsp salt
3½ tsp dried yeast
1 large egg, beaten

METHOD
1. Put the brown ale, butter and honey into a large saucepan and bring to the boil. Set aside until it reaches body temperature (37°C/98.6°F).
2. Put the flours and salt into a large mixing bowl and make a well in the centre.
3. Dissolve the yeast in 1 tablespoon of the beer mixture and pour it into the well in the flour. Add the beaten egg and the remainder of the beer liquid.

Mix with your hands until a soft dough is formed.
4. Turn it out onto a lightly floured board and knead for 10 minutes until it is smooth and elastic. Place the dough in a lightly oiled bowl, cover with a damp tea towel and leave to rise for 1 hour or until it has doubled in size.
5. Knock back the dough, then knead for 5 minutes on a floured surface. Shape it into a loaf and place it in a greased 1kg/2¼lb loaf tin. Leave to prove for 30 minutes, covered with a tea towel.
6. Preheat the oven to 200°C/400°F/gas mark 6. Bake the loaf for 30–35 minutes or until it is golden brown and sounds hollow when tapped on the base.
7. Leave the loaf to cool on a wire rack before serving with some soft cheese and smoked ham.

SUN-DRIED TOMATO BREAD

This bread makes a wonderful lunch served slightly warm with some buffalo mozzarella and cured meats.

INGREDIENTS *Makes 1 large loaf*
425g/14½oz strong white
    bread flour
40g/1¼oz Parmesan cheese,
    grated
50g/1¾oz sun-dried tomatoes,
    drained and chopped
3 tbsp sun-dried tomato paste
1 tbsp chopped fresh oregano
1 tbsp chopped fresh rosemary
1 sachet easy-blend yeast
325ml/11fl oz warm water
a few sprigs of fresh rosemary
olive oil reserved from the
    tomatoes
coarse sea salt

METHOD

1. Put the flour, cheese, tomatoes, tomato paste, herbs and yeast into a large bowl and mix. Make a well in the centre and gradually add the water. Mix together with your hands until the dough starts to leave the sides of the bowl.

2. Turn the dough out onto a lightly floured surface and knead for 10 minutes until it is smooth and elastic in texture. Shape into a 23cm/9in round and place on a greased baking tray.

3. Make some dents in the top of the dough with your fingers and press a few sprigs of rosemary into the surface. Drizzle with the reserved olive oil and sprinkle generously with coarse sea salt. Cover with a damp tea towel and leave to rise for 45 minutes or until it has doubled in size.

4. Preheat the oven to 220°C/425°F/gas mark 7. Place the loaf in the oven, reduce the heat to 200°C/400°F/gas mark 6 and bake for 35 minutes or until golden brown. Cool on a wire rack before serving.

CHEESE & ONION ROLLS

As they cook, the smell of these cheesy rolls is so tempting that you may find it impossible to leave them to cool before eating!

INGREDIENTS *Makes 12 rolls*

15g/½oz butter

1 tbsp olive oil

1 onion, finely chopped

FOR THE BREAD:

2 tsp dried yeast

360ml/12fl oz warm water

450g/1lb strong white bread flour

60g/2oz sugar

½ tsp salt

1 egg, beaten

30g/1oz butter, melted

115g/4oz Cheddar cheese, grated

FOR THE GLAZE:

1 egg, beaten with 3 tbsp milk

METHOD

1. Start by melting the butter and oil in a frying pan. Add the chopped onion and fry over a low heat, stirring regularly, for about 10 minutes until translucent, being careful not to let it brown. Drain on kitchen paper and set aside.

2. Dissolve the yeast in 120ml/ 4fl oz of warm water. Leave the mixture until it is bubbly and has a froth on the surface.

3. Put the flour, sugar and salt in a large bowl and make a well in the centre. Add the yeast mixture, beaten egg, melted butter and the remainder of the water a little at a time until you have a smooth dough.

4. Turn the dough out onto a lightly floured surface and knead for 8–10 minutes. Put the dough into a lightly oiled bowl, cover with a damp tea towel and leave to rise for 1 hour or until it has doubled in size.

5. Knock back the dough and then chafe lightly for 2 minutes to incorporate the grated cheese into the dough. Divide the dough into 12 equal pieces and roll them under the palm of your hand to produce rounds.

6. Put the rolls on greased baking trays, allowing at least 5cm/2in between each one. Cover with a damp tea towel and leave to rise for 30 minutes.

7. Preheat the oven to 200°C/400°F/gas mark 6.

8. Brush the top of each roll with the beaten egg and milk glaze and sprinkle with the cooked onions.

9. Bake in the preheated oven for 15–20 minutes or until the rolls are golden brown. Transfer to a wire rack to cool.

VARIATION

For a tasty breakfast roll, substitute 175g/6oz smoked bacon for the onion. Fry the bacon until it is crispy, then allow to cool. Chop into small pieces and incorporate it into the dough in Step 5, instead of the grated cheese. Now continue as for the cheese and onion rolls. After glazing the rolls, sprinkle them with grated cheese instead of onion.

CHEESE & POTATO ROLLS

These are lovely crusty rolls that make a great accompaniment
to a steaming bowl of homemade soup.

INGREDIENTS *Makes 16 rolls*
450g/1lb floury potatoes, peeled
    and boiled
150ml/5fl oz whole milk
100g/3½oz goat's cheese
675g/1½lb strong white
    bread flour
2 tsp fine sea salt
3½ tsp dried yeast
420ml/14½fl oz warm water

METHOD
1. Mash the potatoes with the
milk and cheese until smooth.
2. Put the flour and salt in a
large bowl and make a well
in the centre.
3. Dissolve the yeast in 2
tablespoons of warm water and
leave until it starts to bubble.
4. Add the yeast and the potato
mixture to the flour. Gradually
add the remaining water and
mix with your hands until

you have a soft dough.
5. Turn out onto a lightly floured
surface and knead for 10–15
minutes until it is smooth and
elastic. Place in a lightly oiled
bowl, cover with a damp tea
towel and leave to rise for 1 hour
or until it has doubled in size.
6. Knock back the dough and
knead for a further 2–3 minutes.
Divide into 16 equal pieces and
shape into rounds, making a
cross in the top of each one with
a sharp knife. Place on greased
baking trays, allowing plenty of
space for them to rise. Lightly
dust with extra flour, cover and
leave to prove for 20 minutes.
7. Bake in a preheated oven
at 220°C/425°F/gas mark 7 for
10 minutes. Reduce the heat to
190°C/375°F/gas mark 5 and bake
for a further 15 minutes, or until
the rolls are golden brown.

TIGER BREAD

Tiger bread has become very popular on the supermarket shelves in recent years, but nothing will beat this homemade version.

INGREDIENTS *Makes 1 large loaf*
450g/1lb strong white bread flour
3 tsp sugar
2 tsp salt
1 sachet easy-blend yeast
300ml/10 fl oz warm water

FOR THE GLAZE:
2 tbsp rice flour
2 tbsp toasted sesame seed oil

METHOD
1. Mix the flour, sugar, salt and yeast in a large bowl and make a well in the centre. Add the warm water a little at a time, mixing until the dough comes away from the sides of the bowl.
2. Turn the dough out onto a lightly floured surface and knead for 5 minutes or until it is smooth and elastic. Place it in a lightly oiled bowl, cover with a damp tea towel and leave to rise for 1 hour, or until doubled in size.
3. Knock back the dough and then knead for a further 5 minutes on a lightly floured surface until it feels soft and pliable. Shape the dough into a large oval and place it on a greased baking sheet.
4. Preheat the oven to 220°C/425°F/gas mark 7.
5. Mix the rice flour and sesame oil together to form a smooth paste. Using a knife, spread the paste over the top of the loaf until it covers the surface. Cover with a damp tea towel and leave to rise for 10–15 minutes or until it has doubled in size.
6. Cook in the preheated oven for 25–30 minutes or until the rice flour topping has gone brown and started to crack.
7. Remove from the oven and leave to cool on a wire rack.

SPELT BREAD

Spelt is closely related to wheat but contains more protein and has a slightly nuttier, sweeter flavour.

INGREDIENTS *Makes 1 large loaf*
450g/1lb white or wholegrain
   spelt flour
½ tsp salt
1 sachet easy-blend yeast
1 tsp sugar
300ml/10fl oz warm water
1 tbsp vegetable oil

METHOD
1. Mix together the flour, salt, yeast and sugar in a large bowl and make a well in the centre. Gradually add the water and mix together with your hands.
2. While the mixture is still quite coarse, add the oil and mix until it feels smooth. Turn the dough out onto a lightly floured surface and knead for about 10 minutes or until it feels soft and elastic in texture.
3. Cover the dough with a damp tea towel and leave to rise in a warm place for 1 hour or until it has doubled in volume.
4. Knock back the dough and knead for a further 3–4 minutes.
5. Grease a 900g/2lb bread tin with butter and put the dough in it. Cover with a damp tea towel and leave to rise for 25 minutes in a warm place.
6. Preheat the oven to 220°C/425°F/gas mark 7.
7. Remove the tea towel and bake the loaf in the oven for 35–40 minutes or until golden brown. The loaf should sound hollow when tapped on the base.
8. Remove from the tin and leave to cool on a wire rack.

Spelt flour contains gluten so is not suitable for people who are gluten intolerant. However, it can be tolerated by some people who cannot eat wheat.

ANISE CROWN BREAD

This circular loaf looks wonderful as a centrepiece at the end of a meal, served with an assortment of cheeses.

INGREDIENTS *Makes 1 large loaf*

1 tsp anise seeds

270ml/9fl oz water

1 tbsp clear honey

270ml/9fl oz whole milk, warmed

1 tsp dried yeast

500g/1lb 2oz strong white
   bread flour

3 tsp salt

2 tbsp olive oil

1 beaten egg, to glaze

METHOD

1. Put the anise and water in a saucepan and boil for 5 minutes. Remove from the heat, add the honey and milk and leave to cool to 37°C/98.6°F.

2. Sprinkle the yeast over the liquid and stir until dissolved.

3. Put the flour and salt in a large bowl, make a well in the centre and pour in the liquid. Mix with your hands until you have a soft dough. Turn it out onto a floured surface and knead for 10 minutes. Keep some flour handy in case the dough gets too sticky.

4. Put the dough into a bowl and drizzle it with the olive oil. Cover with a damp tea towel and leave in a warm place for 1 hour or until it has doubled in size.

5. Knock back the dough and knead for a further 2 minutes. Roll the dough under the palms of your hands into a 28cm/11in rope. Twist the rope several times and then pinch the two ends together and tuck underneath.

6. Place the crown on a greased baking tray, cover and leave to prove for 30 minutes.

7. Preheat the oven to 200°C/400°F/gas mark 6. Brush the dough with the beaten egg and bake for 30 minutes. Cool on a wire rack.

HERBY PLAIT

The herbs in this bread complement the combination of wheat, rye and malted barley in the country grain flour.

INGREDIENTS *Makes 1 large loaf*
675g/1½lb country grain
    bread flour
1 tsp fine salt
1 tsp sugar
1 sachet easy-blend yeast
50g/1¾oz mixed fresh herbs
    (basil, parsley, oregano),
    finely chopped
15g/½oz white vegetable fat,
    diced
360ml/12fl oz warm water
1 egg, beaten, for glazing
1 tbsp poppy or sesame
    seeds (optional)

METHOD
1. Mix together the flour, salt, sugar, yeast and herbs in a large bowl. Add the vegetable fat and work it into the flour with your fingertips until the mixture has the consistency of breadcrumbs. Make a well in the centre and

gradually add the warm water until the dough is smooth and comes away from the sides of the bowl cleanly.

2. Turn the dough out onto a lightly floured surface and knead for 10 minutes or until it is smooth and elastic in texture. Cover with a damp tea towel and leave in a warm place for 1 hour or until it has doubled in size.

3. Knock back the dough and knead lightly for 2 minutes on a lightly floured surface.

4. To plait the dough, flour your hands and then divide the dough into 3 equal pieces. Roll the pieces of dough under the palms of your hands until you have three rope shapes about 30cm/12in long. Leave the dough for 10 minutes to allow it to relax into its proper shape.

5. Wet one end of each of the

ropes with water then pinch them together to seal and fold them underneath. Plait the three pieces just as you would if you were plaiting hair; pull the left piece over the middle one, then hold the former middle piece with your left hand and pull it to the side. Next, bring the right piece over the new middle piece. Repeat this process, alternating sides, until you have plaited the entire length.

6. Wet the ends of the pieces of the plait with water, press them together with your fingers and then secure them underneath the loaf.

7. Place the finished loaf on a greased baking tray, cover with a damp tea towel and leave to rise for about 45 minutes or until it has doubled in size.

8. Preheat the oven to 190°C/375°F/gas mark 5.

9. Prepare a glaze by beating the egg with a little water. When the dough has finished rising, remove the tea towel and gently brush the glaze over the entire surface of the loaf. Sprinkle with poppy or sesame seeds, if using.

10. Bake the bread in the centre of the oven for 20 minutes, then cover it with a large sheet of kitchen foil to protect the top. Continue to bake for a further 15 minutes or until the crust is a deep golden brown.

11. Transfer the loaf to a wire rack to cool.

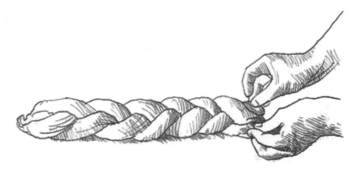

OLIVE SWIRLS

This is a savoury version of cinnamon swirls, with a rich texture and wonderful salty tang.

INGREDIENTS *Makes 12 swirls*
450g/1lb strong white bread flour
1 tsp salt
1 sachet easy-blend yeast
6 tbsp extra virgin olive oil, plus extra for glazing
300ml/10fl oz warm water
a small bunch of basil
175g/6oz pitted large black olives
1 garlic clove, crushed
60g/2oz pitted green olives

METHOD
1. Mix together the flour, salt and yeast in a large bowl. Make a well in the centre and gradually add 2 tablespoons of the olive oil and the warm water. Mix with your hands until a soft dough is formed.
2. Turn the dough out onto a floured board and knead for 10 minutes. Put the dough in

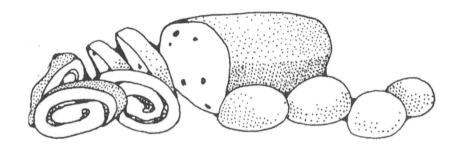

a lightly oiled bowl, cover with a damp tea towel and leave to rise in a warm place for 1 hour, or until it has doubled in size.

2. While the dough is proving, make the filling. Remove the basil leaves from the stalks and put in a mini food processor with the black olives. Add the remaining olive oil and the garlic and whizz to a coarse paste.

3. Preheat the oven to 220°C/425°F/gas mark 7.

4. Line a shallow 30cm × 20cm/ 12in × 8in baking tray with non-stick baking parchment.

5. Knock back the dough and turn it out onto a lightly floured work surface. Using a wooden rolling pin, roll out the dough to a rectangle shape approximately 30cm × 40cm/12in × 16in. Spread the olive paste all over the dough. Arrange the whole green olives in a line along one of the short sides. Roll up the dough like a Swiss roll, starting at the end where the whole olives are and making a long sausage shape.

6. Cut the dough into 12 slices, then carefully slide a spatula underneath them and place them on the lined baking tray, leaving at least 5cm/2in between each one.

7. Brush the top of each swirl with a little olive oil, loosely cover with a damp tea towel and leave to rise in a warm place for 20 minutes. They will not double in size but they should puff up nicely.

8. Bake in the preheated oven for 20–25 minutes until golden. Leave them to cool in the tray before serving.

NEED TO KNOW

The only difference between green and black olives is that green olives are unripe, whereas black ones are fully ripe. There are many varieties, so choose your favourite for this recipe.

BLACK PEPPER & FIG BREAD

This loaf can be made with white or wholemeal flour and
is wonderful with cheese.

INGREDIENTS *Makes 1 large loaf*
650g/1lb 6oz strong white
    bread flour
2 tsp freshly ground black pepper
2 tsp salt
1 sachet easy-blend yeast
2 tbsp olive oil
420ml/14½fl oz warm water
350g/12oz dried figs, chopped

METHOD
1. Combine the flour, pepper, salt
and yeast in a large bowl. Make
a well in the middle and add
the olive oil. Gradually add the
water and mix with your hands
until you have a soft dough.
2. Turn the dough out onto a
lightly floured surface and knead
for 10 minutes until it is smooth
and elastic in texture.
3. Put the dough in a lightly oiled
bowl, cover with a damp tea
towel and leave in a warm place
for 1 hour or until it has doubled
in size.
4. Knock back the dough and
then turn it out onto a lightly
floured surface. Add the chopped
figs to the dough and gently
chafe until they are mixed
throughout the dough. Do not
overwork at this stage – it does
not matter if the dough looks a
little rough. Shape the dough
into a rough oval and place on
a lightly greased and floured
baking tray. With a sharp knife,
make some diagonal cuts in the
top of the loaf then dust with
flour. Leave to rise, uncovered,
for about 10–15 minutes.
5. Bake in a preheated oven at
200°C/400°F/gas mark 6 for 40–45
minutes or until the loaf is brown
and sounds hollow when tapped
underneath. Leave to cool on a
wire rack before serving.

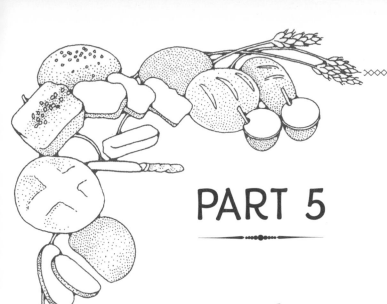

PART 5

FLAT BREADS

Until the discovery of raising agents, all bread was unleavened, or flat. Different countries have produced their own versions of flatbread, and there are many to choose from – for example, pitta, naan, focaccia, chapatti – not forgetting that perennial favourite, pizza.

FLAT BREADS

Many flat breads consist of just three simple ingredients – flour, water and salt – although some, such as pizza dough and Indian naan bread, require a raising agent.

PIZZA

Famous as an Italian dish, pizza is now found worldwide and is a favourite with both young and old. Pizza, as we know it today, follows the Italian tradition of layering tomato sauce on a dough base and topping it with extra ingredients such as cheese, olives, meat, fish, or indeed anything you fancy.

Surprising though it may seem, pizza was not an Italian creation. It is believed the Ancient Greeks were the first people to bake a round, flat bread which they topped with items such as spices, olives, potatoes and anything else that was available at the time. However, the pizza we all recognize today originated in Naples, in the 18th century.

TOMATO SAUCE

For the basic tomato sauce use the following ingredients:

2 tbsp extra virgin olive oil
1 onion, finely chopped
2 cloves garlic, finely chopped
1 bay leaf
1 tsp dried oregano
400g/14oz can chopped tomatoes
2 tbsp tomato purée
salt and black pepper

Heat the olive oil in a saucepan and gently cook the onion and garlic for about 8 minutes or until they are soft and translucent. Add the remaining ingredients and simmer for 10 minutes or until you have a thick sauce. Season with salt and pepper and remove the bay leaf.

PIZZA DOUGH

This recipe gives a crisp, tasty base and doesn't
take too long to rise.

INGREDIENTS *Makes 2 pizzas*
250g/9oz strong white bread flour
1 tsp salt
1 tsp dried yeast
60ml/2fl oz warm water

METHOD
1. Mix the flour and salt in a
large bowl and make a well in
the middle. Dissolve the yeast in
the warm water and then add to
the flour. Mix with your hands,
gradually bringing in the flour
from the sides of the bowl until
you have a fairly rough dough.
2. Turn the dough out onto a
lightly floured suirface and
knead for 10 minutes. Place the
dough in a lightly oiled bowl,
cover with a damp tea towel and
leave to rise for 1 hour.
3. Knock back the dough and
knead it for another 10 minutes
on a lightly floured surface.

Return it to the bowl and leave to
prove for another hour.
4. Preheat the oven to 220°C/
425°F/gas mark 7.
5. Knock back the dough for
a second time then turn it out
onto a lightly floured surface.
Divide the dough in half and
roll each half into a ball with
your hands. Use a rolling pin to
press the dough flat until you
have 2 circles about 30cm/12in
in diameter. Place them on a
lightly greased baking sheet or
traditional pizza stone.
6. Spread tomato sauce (see
opposite) over each base and
add your favourite toppings.
7. Place the pizzas in the
preheated oven and cook for
12–15 minutes or until the topping
is bubbling and the edges of the
dough are starting to go brown.
Serve immediately.

CALZONE

Calzone, meaning 'stocking', is simply a stuffed pizza.
It makes a wonderful, filling meal.

INGREDIENTS *Makes 3 calzones*
1 recipe for pizza dough (see
    page 83)
1 egg, beaten

FOR THE FILLING:
1 aubergine, peeled and diced
sea salt and freshly ground
    black pepper
2 tbsp olive oil
1 onion, finely chopped
150g/5½oz minced pork
1 garlic clove, finely chopped
6 large tomatoes, skinned,
    seeded and chopped
1 tbsp tomato purée
1 tsp dried oregano
1 tsp dried sage
200g/7oz mozzarella cheese,
    broken into pieces

METHOD
1. Spread the diced aubergine
on a large baking sheet, sprinkle
with salt and leave for 10
minutes. Rinse and then dry
with kitchen paper.
2. Heat the olive oil in a large
frying pan over a medium heat
and cook the onion until it is soft
but not brown. Add the pork and
cook until it is lightly browned,
about 5 minutes.
3. Add the aubergine and garlic
and cook for a further 5 minutes,
stirring frequently.
4. Add the tomatoes, tomato
purée and herbs and season
with salt and pepper. Cook for 20
minutes or until the mixture has
thickened. Set aside.
5. Preheat the oven to 200°C/
400°F/gas mark 6.
6. Knead the pizza dough on a
lightly floured surface for 2–3
minutes, then divide it into 6
equal pieces. Shape each piece
into a ball with your hands.

Using a rolling pin, roll out circles approximately 25cm/10in in diameter and to a thickness of 1cm/½in.

7. Place 3 of the circles on lightly greased and floured baking trays and spread some of the filling over the top, leaving about 2.5cm/1in around the edge. Dot pieces of mozzarella cheese over the filling.

8. Brush the edges with the beaten egg then top with the remaining 3 dough circles. Press the edges down firmly, using a fork.

9. Make a slash in the top of each calzone with a sharp knife, brush with olive oil and bake in the preheated oven for 20 minutes or until the edges are golden brown.

10. Remove the calzone from the oven, cut in half and serve immediately. Remember – the filling will be very hot.

VEGGIE VARIATION

1 onion, finely chopped
1 garlic clove, finely
    chopped
450g/1lb young spinach
    leaves
1 mild red chilli, deseeded
    and chopped
2 tbsp chopped sun-dried
    tomatoes
1 tbsp olive oil
3 tbsp freshly grated
    Parmesan cheese
150g/5½oz ricotta cheese

Fry the onion and garlic until soft. Add the spinach, chilli and tomatoes and cook until the spinach has wilted. Add the cheeses and season with salt and pepper.

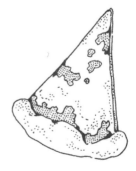

CLASSIC FOCACCIA

This is an easy version of the traditional Italian focaccia – a light flat bread enriched with olive oil and flavoured with rosemary.

INGREDIENTS *Makes 1 round loaf*
225g/8oz strong white bread flour
1 tsp salt
2 tsp dried yeast
185ml/6½fl oz warm water
4 tbsp olive oil
1 garlic clove, crushed
coarse sea salt
4 sprigs of fresh rosemary

METHOD

1. Place the flour in a mound on a clean work surface or large board. Sprinkle on the salt and make a well in the centre of the mound. Dissolve the yeast in a little of the water, then add this mixture to the well. Carefully fold the flour over the top of the hollow, then gradually add 3 tablespoons of olive oil to the mixture. Working the mixture with your hands, gradually add enough of the remaining water until you have a stiff but pliable dough.

2. Knead the dough on a lightly floured surface for 10–15 minutes. Put the dough into a lightly oiled bowl, cover with a damp tea towel and leave in a warm place for about 30 minutes or until it has doubled in size.

3. Preheat the oven to 220°C/425°F/gas mark 7.

4. Brush a baking tray with olive oil. Put the garlic clove in

a tablespoon of olive oil and set aside to steep.

5. Knock back the dough, then knead it for a further 2–3 minutes on a lightly floured surface. Make it into a ball with your hands and then, using a rolling pin, flatten and roll it out into a circle about 5mm/¼in thick.

6. Place the dough on the greased baking tray and make some indentations in the surface using your fingertips. Brush the surface with the garlic-infused olive oil using a soft-bristled pastry brush. Sprinkle the surface with coarse sea salt then break off some leaves from the rosemary sprigs and push them into each of the indentations.

7. Bake for 10 minutes in the preheated oven, then reduce the temperature to 190°C/375°F/gas mark 5 and bake for a further 20 minutes. This bread is best served hot.

VARIATIONS

Here are some suggestions for different toppings for your focaccia.

• Add sage or any other herb of your choice in place of the rosemary.

• Sweat some chopped onions in a little olive oil until they are translucent and spread on top of the focaccia before baking.

• Chop some black and green olives in half and push one half into each indentation before baking.

• Top with slices of fresh tomato and sprinkle with mixed herbs and black pepper.

• Chop some anchovies, oregano and garlic and spread over the top before baking.

PITTA BREAD

This versatile flat bread can be sliced and served with dips or split open and filled with different ingredients such as cheese and salad.

INGREDIENTS *Makes 8 pittas*
250g/9oz strong white bread flour
250g/9oz wholemeal flour
1 tsp salt
2 tsp dried yeast
½ tsp granulated sugar
300ml/10fl oz warm water
2 tbsp olive oil

METHOD

1. Mix the flours and salt together in a large bowl. Dissolve the yeast and sugar in a little of the warm water. Make a well in the centre of the flour and add the yeast mixture, olive oil and enough of the remaining water to make a firm but soft dough.

2. Turn the dough out onto a lightly floured surface and knead for about 15 minutes or until it is smooth and elastic in texture. Place the dough in a lightly oiled bowl, cover with a damp tea towel and leave to rise in a warm place for 1½ hours or until it has doubled in size.

3. Knock back the dough, knead for 2–3 minutes, then cover and prove for 10 minutes.

4. Divide the dough into 8 equal pieces and shape each one into a ball with your hands. Roll out on a lightly floured surface to the characteristic pitta oval, about 23cm/9in in length and 5mm/¼in thick. Cover and leave to prove for 20 minutes.

5. Preheat the oven to 220°C/ 425°F/gas mark 7. Lightly dust 2 baking trays with flour and preheat in the oven for 5 minutes. Place the pittas on the hot baking trays and bake for 5–10 minutes or until they are puffed up. Wrap in a clean, dry tea towel when cooked to keep the crusts soft, as they can dry out very quickly.

NAAN BREAD

This Indian flat bread was traditionally baked in a clay tandoor oven. It has been adapted here to cook on the barbecue.

INGREDIENTS *Makes 14 naans*
1 sachet easy-blend yeast
240ml/8fl oz warm water
4 tbsp caster sugar
3 tbsp semi-skimmed milk
1 egg, beaten
1 tsp salt
800g/1¾lb strong white
    bread flour
50g/2oz butter, melted

METHOD
1. Dissolve the yeast in the warm water and leave to stand for 10 minutes until frothy. Put the sugar, milk, egg, salt and flour in a large bowl and add the yeast mixture. Mix with your hands until it forms a soft dough. Turn it out onto a lightly floured surface and knead for 6–8 minutes until smooth. Place the dough in a well oiled bowl, cover with a damp tea towel and leave to rise for 1 hour in a warm place until it has doubled in volume.

2. Knock back the dough, then knead for 2–3 minutes. Break off pieces of dough about the size of a golf ball and roll them into balls. Place them on a baking tray, cover with a cloth and leave to rise for 30 minutes or until doubled in size.

3. Preheat the barbecue until the coals are glowing red and paint the griddle with a little oil to stop the bread from sticking.

4. Roll out the dough balls in thin circles, then cook for 2–3 minutes on one side until they are puffy and lightly browned. Brush the uncooked side with butter, turn the naan over and cook for another 2–3 minutes, until browned on this side, too. Serve the naan with curry and pieces of barbecued chicken.

MEXICAN TORTILLAS

Next time you fancy a tortilla wrap, have a go at making your own;
this recipe is simple and fun to do with children.

INGREDIENTS *Makes 12 wraps*
450g/1lb plain flour
½ tsp baking powder
½ tsp salt
100g/3½oz lard, cut into
    small pieces
120ml/4fl oz warm water

METHOD
1. Sieve the flour, baking
powder and salt into a large
bowl. Add the lard and work
with your fingertips as though
making pastry, until the mixture
resembles rough breadcrumbs.

2. Gradually add the warm water
and keep mixing with your
hands until you have a stiff but
pliable dough.
3. Turn the dough out onto a
lightly floured surface and knead
for 10–15 minutes or until it is
smooth and elastic in texture.
4. Divide the dough into 12 equal-
sized pieces. Using a rolling pin,
roll out each piece until you have
a 30cm/12in circle. Cover the
circles with cling film to prevent
them drying out.
5. Heat a heavy-based frying pan
or griddle and cook each tortilla
for 1 minute on each side. The
surface should turn brown and
start to puff up in places with
air bubbles.
6. As each tortilla is cooked, wrap
it in a clean tea towel to keep
it warm until you have cooked
them all. Fill as desired.

BLACK PEPPER FLAT BREAD

This flat bread is great for picnics, or can be eaten warm with some Parma ham and hard-boiled eggs.

INGREDIENTS *Makes 1 loaf*
350g/12oz strong white
   bread flour
2 tsp salt
1 sachet easy-blend yeast
250ml/8fl oz warm water
4 tbsp butter, melted, plus extra
   for basting
3 tsp freshly ground black pepper

METHOD

1. Mix the flour, salt and yeast in a large bowl and make a well in the centre. Add the water, 2 tablespoons butter and 2 teaspoons of the pepper and work with your hands until a firm ball is formed.

2. Knead the dough on a floured surface for 10–15 minutes or until smooth and elastic in texture. Lightly oil a bowl, put the dough inside, cover with a damp tea towel and leave to rise for 1 hour.

3. Preheat the oven to 200°C/400°F/gas mark 6. Butter a 25cm/10in round baking tin.

4. Knock back the dough, then knead for a further 2–3 minutes. Shape the dough into a large circle, brush with the remaining butter, then fold in half. Reshape into another circle and sprinkle the surface with the remaining pepper. Knead for 5 minutes or until the ingredients are well mixed.

5. Shape the dough into a circle and press into the tin. Cover with a damp tea towel and leave to rise for 10 minutes.

6. Bake in the preheated oven for 20 minutes or until golden brown. During the cooking time, baste the surface of the dough twice more with melted butter.

7. Leave to cool slightly on a wire rack, but eat while still warm.

CIABATTA

This is another Italian bread, also known as 'slipper' bread. This recipe produces a light, holey, slightly chewy dough.

INGREDIENTS *Makes 2 loaves*

FOR THE STARTER:

¹/₈ tsp dried yeast

7 tbsp warm water

150g/5½oz strong white
    bread flour

FOR THE BREAD:

½ tsp dried yeast

2 tbsp warm milk

280g/10oz strong white
    bread flour

1½ tsp salt

1 tbsp olive oil

150ml/5fl oz warm water

METHOD

1. Make the starter by dissolving the yeast in 2 tablespoons of warm water and leave it to stand for 10 minutes, or until it is creamy and starting to froth. Add the remaining water and the flour. Stir for 4 minutes, then cover the bowl with cling film. Leave the starter at room temperature for at least 12 hours and up to 24 hours.

2. To make the bread, stir together the yeast and warm milk and leave to stand for 10 minutes, or until creamy.

3. In a large bowl, combine the flour and salt, making a well in the centre. Add the starter, yeast mixture, oil and sufficient water to make a soft dough. Turn out onto a lightly floured surface and knead for 10 minutes or until the dough is smooth and elastic in texture.

4. Put the dough in a lightly oiled bowl, cover with a damp tea towel and leave in a warm place to rise for about 1½ hours or until it has doubled in size. After this first rise the dough will be sticky and full of air bubbles.

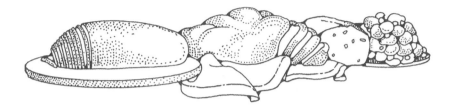

5. Knock back the dough and turn out onto a lightly floured surface. Cut the dough in half and form into rough oval shapes about 25cm/10in long.

6. Put the loaves on 2 baking trays lined with baking parchment and make dimples in the surface using floured fingertips. Dust the tops with flour, cover with a damp tea towel and leave to rise in a warm place for 1½ to 2 hours or until it has doubled in size once again.

7. Preheat the oven to 220°C/ 425°F/gas mark 7.

8. Bake the loaves for 20 minutes or until golden brown. Leave them to cool on a wire rack before serving.

BAKING STONES

Many recipes for ciabatta and pizza suggest the use of a baking stone. Don't be tempted to buy an inexpensive one as it will not absorb enough heat. However, an unglazed quarry tile works extremely well and can be purchased from a DIY store. Place the stone in your oven at least an hour before baking, turning the temperature up as far as it will go. Bread cooked on a stone is extra springy – you will really notice the difference.

RÔTI

Rôti is a soft, flat Indian bread similar to pitta but made with wholemeal flour. It is eaten with curries and other spicy dishes.

INGREDIENTS *Makes 12 rotis*
450g/1lb wholemeal flour
½ tsp salt
½ tsp baking powder
120ml/4fl oz warm water
1 tbsp vegetable oil

METHOD

1. Combine the flour, salt, baking powder, water and oil in a large bowl until the mixture starts to pull away from the sides.

2. Turn the dough out onto a lightly floured surface and knead for 10 minutes until it has a smooth and elastic texture.

3. Heat an ungreased frying pan or griddle to medium high.

4. Divide the dough into 12 equal parts and form into balls with your hands. Cover with a damp cloth to keep them moist.

5. Flatten each ball with the palm of your hand, then roll out with a rolling pin so that the finished rôti is about 20cm/8in in diameter and 3mm/⅛in thick.

6. Cook the rôti on the preheated griddle for 1 minute on each side. It is quite normal for the bread to have some darker brown spots when it has finished cooking.

7. Keep the rôti covered and warm while you cook the remainder and serve while still hot.

RYE CRISPBREAD

Very popular in Scandinavian countries, rye crispbread is easy to make. It's exceptionally tasty and the perfect bread for a snack.

INGREDIENTS *Makes 12*
1 tbsp dried yeast
250ml/8fl oz warm water
125g/4½oz rye flour
150g/5½oz plain flour
1 tsp salt
40g/1½oz dark rye flour

METHOD

1. Sprinkle the yeast into the warm water and set aside for 10 minutes until it goes creamy in colour and develops a froth on the surface.

2. Mix together the rye flour, the plain flour and salt in a large bowl. Make a well in the centre then add the yeast mixture. Using your hands, work in the flour from the sides of the bowl until a soft dough forms.

3. Turn the dough out onto a board or work surface covered with the dark rye flour. Knead lightly for 2–3 minutes until the dark rye flour is incorporated into the dough.

4. Roll the dough under the palm of your hand until you have a fat roll. Slice this into 12 equal-sized portions. Shape each piece into a ball, then place them on a board and cover with a damp towel. Leave to rise in a warm place for 20 minutes.

5. Preheat the oven to 220°C/425°F/gas mark 7. Lightly grease 2 baking trays.

6. On a lightly floured surface, use a rolling pin to roll out each ball into a flat circle 10cm/4in in diameter. Place the circles on the baking trays and prick the surface of each one with a fork.

7. Bake in the preheated oven for 8–10 minutes or until lightly browned. Cool on a wire rack before serving.

BANNOCKS

Bannocks, or oatcakes, were once a traditional part of the Scottish diet and were cooked on a griddle over an open fire.

INGREDIENTS *Makes 8 bannocks*
125g/4½oz medium oatmeal, plus extra for kneading
½ tsp salt
½ tsp bicarbonate of soda
2 tsp lard, melted
scant tbsp hot water

METHOD

1. Mix the oatmeal, salt and bicarbonate of soda in a large bowl. Make a well in the centre and pour in the melted lard. Stir well with a wooden spoon, then add sufficient water to make a stiff paste.

2. Cover your work surface with a thin layer of oatmeal and turn the dough out onto it. You need to work quite quickly at this stage, as the dough is difficult to knead once it cools down.

3. Divide the dough in half and roll into 2 balls. If you find it is sticking to your hands, rub them with some oatmeal. Roll out the dough so that it is about 1cm/½in thick. Place a dinner plate on top of the dough and cut round the edge to make a circle. Cut the circle into quarters (also called farls) and fry them in a preheated, lightly greased frying pan for about 3 minutes, or until the edges start to curl. Turn over and repeat on the other side. Repeat until all the bannocks are cooked.

You can also cook bannocks in the oven at 190°C/375°F/gas mark 5 for about 30 minutes or until they are light brown at the edges. They can be stored in an airtight tin for several days and reheated in a warm oven when you want to use them. Bannocks are really good with cheese.

ROSEMARY & GARLIC FLAT BREAD

Garlic bread makes a wonderful starter, cut into wedges to serve with dips, or as a side dish to accompany your main dish.

INGREDIENTS *Makes 4*
300g/10oz plain flour
60ml/2fl oz yogurt
60ml/2fl oz milk
2 tbsp olive oil
60ml/2fl oz hot water
2 tbsp fresh rosemary leaves
coarse sea salt

GARLIC OIL
2 cloves garlic, finely chopped
3 tbsp olive oil

METHOD
1. Preheat the oven to 230°C/450°F/gas mark 8.
2. Put the flour in a large bowl, make a well in the centre and add the yogurt, milk and olive oil. Gradually add the hot water and mix immediately using a wooden spoon. Work until the dough starts to form a ball.
3. Turn the dough out onto a lightly floured surface and knead for 5 minutes or until it is smooth in texture. Wrap the dough in cling film and leave it at room temperature for 10 minutes.
4. While the dough is resting, make the garlic oil by mixing the chopped garlic and olive oil in a small saucepan. Gently warm the oil over a low heat for 10 minutes then set aside.
5. Divide the dough into 4 pieces and roll into balls. Stretch each ball with your hands until it is an oval or rectangle of about 25.5cm × 13cm/10in × 5in.
6. Line 2 baking trays with baking parchment and place 2 flat breads on each one. Brush with garlic oil and sprinkle with rosemary leaves and sea salt.
7. Bake in the preheated oven for 10–12 minutes.

POTATO FLAT BREAD

This is another popular flat bread eaten in India, where it is called *aloo paratha*. It makes a great breakfast with fried eggs and bacon.

INGREDIENTS *Makes about 12*

2 medium potatoes, peeled and
    cut into pieces
250g/9oz plain flour
1 tbsp vegetable oil
½ tsp salt
1 tsp baking powder
½ tsp ground cumin
¼ tsp sugar
butter, for frying
vegetable oil, for frying

METHOD

1. Boil the potatoes in salted water until soft. Drain them and mash thoroughly.

2. Put the flour into a large bowl, add the vegetable oil, salt, baking powder, cumin and sugar and mix with a wooden spoon. Add the mashed potato and enough water to make a soft dough, using your hands to work the mixture.

3. Break off small pieces of the dough and roll into balls.

4. Lightly flour a work surface and roll each ball into a small circle with a rolling pin.

5. Put a little butter and oil into a heavy-based frying pan and heat until hot but not smoking. Place 1 flat bread in the centre of the pan and tip the pan to make sure the bread is covered in the oil. Cook for about 1–2 minutes or until it starts to go brown. Turn the bread over, add a little more oil and butter and cook until it turns brown.

6. Keep warm while cooking the remaining breads and serve while they are still hot.

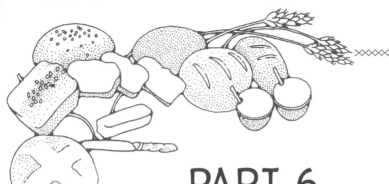

PART 6

GLUTEN-FREE BREADS

Gluten is the ingredient that gives bread its spring and elasticity, so making loaves with gluten-free flours is a little challenging, but it is by no means impossible. Once you become used to cooking the recipes in this section you will find you can achieve some very satisfying results.

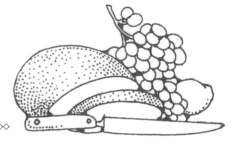

A GLUTEN-FREE DIET

People with coeliac disease, and others who suffer from gluten intolerance, need to find ways of baking that omit gluten. This may seem tricky at first, but soon it becomes second nature.

The principal sources of gluten in the diet are wheat, rye and barley. People with gluten intolerance can eat oats, but usually only in small amounts. For people who are allergic, there are specially prepared gluten-free flours on the market made from alternatives such as rice, soy, buckwheat, corn, potato and even chickpeas.

A gluten-free loaf is much crumblier in texture than a normal loaf, but recipes can be adapted to cope with this. For example, to produce the elastic quality missing in gluten-free flours, you can add a little xanthan gum, which will make the dough easier to handle. You can purchase xanthan gum from most health food stores and certain supermarkets. You can also buy gluten-free baking power, which is available in the baking section in the majority of supermarkets.

Gluten-free bread is quite different in texture to bread made with wheat flour, and it is best served while still warm from the oven – as the bread cools the starch begins to harden and although this does not mean it is stale it is not so nice to eat. Gluten-free bread freezes well, so make a few batches and slice them before freezing. It makes excellent toast and can be used straight from the freezer.

You may find gluten-free dough harder to work with as it is much wetter than dough made with wheat flour, so you might prefer to use a food mixer for these recipes.

SANDWICH LOAF

This gluten-free loaf is simple to make and less crumbly than many of the other recipes.

INGREDIENTS *Makes 2 loaves*

240ml/8fl oz warm water

2 tsp dried yeast

2 tbsp granulated sugar

175g/6oz brown rice flour

85g/3oz ground flax seeds

85g/3oz potato starch

85g/3oz tapioca starch

85g/3oz skimmed milk powder

2½ tsp xanthan gum

1¼ tsp salt

2 tsp apple cider vinegar

2 tbsp vegetable oil

2 eggs, plus 2 extra egg whites

METHOD

1. Mix together the warm water, yeast and sugar in a glass bowl. Stir and leave for 10 minutes until the surface starts to go frothy.

2. Combine all the dry ingredients in a large bowl, mix well with a wooden spoon and set aside.

3. Put the vinegar, oil and eggs in another bowl and beat using a wooden spoon until thoroughly combined. Add the yeast liquid and mix thoroughly.

4. Slowly add the dry ingredients to the batter and mix until they are thoroughly combined. Beat the mixture for about 4–5 minutes using a wooden spoon, or place it in a mixer on the lowest setting.

5. Grease two 450g/1lb bread tins and spoon half the mixture into each. Leave in a warm place, uncovered, to rise for 30–40 minutes or until the dough has risen to the top of the tins.

7. Preheat the oven to 180°C/350°F/gas mark 4. Bake the loaves for 35–45 minutes or until they sound hollow when tapped on the base. Slice and eat while still warm.

PIZZA BASE

You don't have to miss out on making pizzas just because you have a special diet; try this recipe and add your favourite topping.

INGREDIENTS *Makes 4 bases*
1 tsp sugar
15g/½oz dried yeast
250ml/8fl oz warm water
175g/6oz rice flour, plus extra for dusting
85g/3oz potato flour
50g/1¾oz tapioca flour
30g/1oz dried milk
1½ tsp gluten-free baking powder
1 tsp xanthan gum
1 tsp salt
1 tbsp sunflower oil
1 egg

METHOD

1. Dissolve the sugar and yeast in half of the warm water and leave in a warm place for 10 minutes or until the mixture has become frothy.

2. Combine the flours, dried milk, baking powder, xanthan gum and salt in a bowl.

3. In a separate bowl, whisk together the oil and egg and gradually add the dry ingredients. Add the yeast mixture and the remaining water and work with your hands for 3–4 minutes until you achieve a smooth dough. Alternatively, use a food processor with a 'K' blade fitted and work the dough for 3–4 minutes on medium speed.

4. Turn the dough out onto a surface sprinkled with rice flour and rub some flour on your hands as it will be sticky. Divide the dough into 4 equal parts.

5. Line a baking tray with baking parchment and place one piece of the dough on top. Using the heel of your hand, flatten the dough until you have a circle measuring about 20cm/8in in diameter. Repeat this with the 3 remaining pieces.

6. Cover the dough with clean tea towels and leave to rise in a warm place for 15 minutes.
7. Preheat the oven to 200°C/400°F/gas mark 6.
8. Bake the bases in the oven for 8–10 minutes before taking out of the oven and adding tomato sauce (see page 82) and your favourite toppings (see suggestions, right). Return the pizzas to the oven and bake for a further 10–15 minutes or until the bases are crisp and the toppings bubbling. Serve immediately.

If you do not wish to use all the bases at once, they freeze well as complete pizzas with toppings.

GLUTEN-FREE PIZZA TOPPINGS

- mushrooms, sliced
  tomatoes, sliced
  red peppers, sliced
  1 garlic clove, chopped
  pepperoni, sliced
  cheddar cheese, grated

- spinach, wilted
  fennel, thinly sliced
  4 garlic cloves, roasted
  butternut squash, roasted
  mozzarella cheese, broken into pieces

- tomatoes, chopped
  1 red onion, caramelized
  mushrooms, sliced
  basil leaves
  Italian sausage, sliced
  mozzarella cheese, grated

- tomatoes, chopped
  tomato purée
  mushrooms, sliced
  red chilli, sliced

CIABATTA

A taste of Italy fresh from the oven which can rival any traditional ciabatta for flavour.

INGREDIENTS *Makes 1 small loaf*
1 tbsp sunflower oil
225g/8oz gluten-free white flour
4 tsp gluten-free baking powder
¼ tsp xanthan gum
1 egg
½ tsp sea salt flakes
250–270ml/8–9fl oz warm water

METHOD
1. Preheat the oven to 200°C/ 400°F/gas mark 6.
2. Lightly grease a 450g/1lb loaf tin with sunflower oil.
3. Put the flour, baking powder, xanthan gum, egg and sea salt into a food processor. Pour in most of the water, leaving about 30ml/1fl oz remaining. Process until you have a smooth, runny dough.
4. If the mixture looks a little too firm at this stage, add the remainder of the water and mix until smooth and creamy.
5. Pour the batter into the prepared loaf tin, level off the top with the blade of a knife and bake in the preheated oven for 25 minutes or until golden brown.
6. Remove the ciabatta from the oven. Leave to cool on a wire rack until it is just warm and then serve immediately.

CRUMPETS

These are a real treat and very hard to distinguish from those made with wheat. Toast them before serving with your favourite topping.

INGREDIENTS *Makes 12 crumpets*
1 tsp dried yeast
330ml/11fl oz warm water
300g/10oz gluten-free self-raising
   flour
30–40ml/1–1½fl oz apple juice
   concentrate
vegetable oil, for greasing

METHOD
1. Dissolve the yeast in the warm water and set aside for 5 minutes.
2. Sift the flour into a large bowl.
3. Add the yeast mixture and apple juice to the flour and beat until you have a smooth consistency.

4. Brush metal crumpet rings with oil and heat them in a heavy-based frying pan.
5. Fill the rings three-quarters full with the batter and cook on a medium heat for 8–10 minutes or until holes start to appear in the surface and the batter has just dried out.
6. Remove the crumpet rings carefully using a kitchen towel or a pair of tongs, turn the crumpets over and cook for a further 2 minutes on the other side.
7. Transfer the crumpets to a wire rack to cool while you cook the remaining batter.

BANANA BREAD

The addition of bananas to this bread means it stays moist and will keep in the fridge for up to a week.

INGREDIENTS *Makes 1 large loaf*
85g/3oz butter
175g/6oz golden caster sugar
2 eggs, beaten
450g/1lb bananas, mashed
200g/7oz gluten-free flour
¼ tsp bicarbonate of soda
115g/4oz grated carrot

METHOD

1. Grease and line a 900g/2lb loaf tin. Preheat the oven to 180°C/350°F/gas mark 4.
2. Cream the butter and sugar together in a bowl until they are pale in colour and fluffy.
3. Add the eggs one at a time, beating well after each.
4. Add the mashed bananas and beat again for a couple of minutes.
5. Stir in the flour, bicarbonate of soda and grated carrot, taking care not to knock the air out of the mixture.
6. Put the mixture into the prepared loaf tin and bake in the centre of the oven for 1¼ hours or until well-risen and firm. You can test whether the bread is fully cooked by inserting a skewer into the centre – if it comes out clean the bread is ready. If the skewer comes out with some uncooked mixture on it, return the bread to the oven and cook for a little longer.
7. Turn the bread out onto a wire rack to cool and serve sliced and spread with butter.

MARMALADE BREAKFAST LOAF

This bread has a wonderful tangy flavour and makes a lovely change for breakfast or a mid-morning snack.

INGREDIENTS *Makes 1 large loaf*
500g/1lb 2oz gluten-free white
   flour
1 sachet easy-blend yeast
1 tbsp dried semi-skimmed milk
200ml/7fl oz hot water (just boiled)
150ml/5fl oz freshly squeezed
   orange juice
60g/2oz butter, melted
125g/4½oz thin shred marmalade

FOR THE GLAZE:
15g/½oz butter, melted
2 tbsp caster sugar
2 tbsp orange juice

METHOD
1. Grease and line a 900g/2lb loaf tin.
2. Combine the dry ingredients in a large bowl and make a well in the centre. Add the water, orange juice, melted butter and marmalade to the well and beat with a wooden spoon until you have a smooth, runny batter.
2. Spoon the batter into the prepared loaf tin. Cover with oiled cling film and leave in a warm place to prove for about 1 hour, or until the batter has almost reached the top of the tin.
4. Preheat the oven to 190°C/375°F/gas mark 5.
5. Once the batter has risen, remove the cling film, place the loaf in the centre of the preheated oven and bake for 1 hour until it has risen and turned golden brown. Cover loosely with kitchen foil for the last 20 minutes of cooking to stop the top from burning.
6. Mix the ingredients for the glaze together. Remove the loaf from the oven, turn it out onto a wire rack and brush with the glaze while it is still warm.

BROWN SODA BREAD

This gluten-free soda bread uses a combination of white and brown flour to give a moist, nutty-flavoured loaf.

INGREDIENTS *Makes 1 large loaf*
250g/9oz gluten-free brown flour
250g/9oz gluten-free white flour
¼ tsp salt
1 tbsp gluten-free baking powder
2 tsp xanthan gum
1 tsp white wine vinegar
1 tbsp vegetable oil
500ml/16fl oz rice milk, plus extra
2 tbsp

METHOD
1. Preheat the oven to 200°C/400°F/gas mark 6. Grease a 450g/1lb loaf tin.
2. Mix together the flours, salt, baking powder and xanthan gum in a large bowl and make a well in the centre.
3. Combine the vinegar, oil and milk in a jug and add to the flour mixture. Stir until you have a soft, slightly sticky dough.
4. Dust your hands in gluten-free flour and roughly shape the dough to fit it into the loaf tin. Brush the top of the dough with the additional milk.
5. Bake the loaf in the centre of the preheated oven for 1½–1¾ hours or until it is golden brown and sounds hollow when tapped on the base.
6. Turn out onto a wire rack and leave to cool before slicing.

VARIATION

A delicious variation on this soda bread is the addition of 150g/5½oz large, juicy raisins and the grated zest of 1 orange. Add to the dry ingredients before mixing.

HONEY & SUNFLOWER SEED LOAF

This delicious, moist loaf is irresistible when sliced, lightly buttered and served with chopped banana.

INGREDIENTS *Makes 1 small loaf*
250g/9oz gluten-free white flour
1 sachet easy-blend yeast
¼ tsp salt
30g/1oz butter
120ml/4fl oz milk
90ml/3fl oz water
1 tbsp clear honey
40g/1¼oz sunflower seeds

METHOD
1. Grease a 450g/1lb non-stick loaf tin.
2. Put the flour, yeast and salt into a large bowl and make a well in the centre.
3. Melt the butter in a small saucepan, remove from the heat and add the milk, water and honey. While the liquid is still warm, add it to the dry ingredients and beat well until you have a smooth batter. Stir in half the sunflower seeds.

4. Spoon the batter into the prepared loaf tin. Cover with oiled cling film and leave in a warm place to rise for about 1 hour, or until the mixture reaches the top of the tin.
5. Preheat the oven to 200°C/ 400°F/gas mark 6.
6. Once the dough has risen sufficiently, remove the cling film and sprinkle with the remainder of the sunflower seeds.
7. Bake in the preheated oven for 20–25 minutes or until the loaf is golden brown and sounds hollow when tapped on the base.
8. Remove the loaf from the tin and leave to cool on a wire rack before slicing.

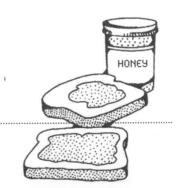

LINSEED, DATE & RAISIN BREAD

Linseed and buckwheat are used to replace the gluten in this recipe for a sweet breakfast or tea loaf.

INGREDIENTS *Makes 1 loaf*

150g/5½oz buckwheat grains
    combined with 2 tbsp linseed,
    soaked for 3 hours
225g/8oz dried dates, soaked for
    3 hours
50g/1¾oz butter, melted
75g/2½oz raisins
2 tbsp linseed combined with
    8 tbsp of water and soaked for
    3 hours
40g/1¼oz rice flour
2 tsp gluten-free baking powder
coconut milk, to adjust batter to a
    dropping consistency

METHOD

1. Preheat the oven to 180°C/ 350°F/gas mark 4. Grease and line a 450g/1lb loaf tin.

2. Drain the combined soaked linseed and buckwheat grains and place in a blender. Blend until you have a smooth paste.

3. Drain the soaked dates and blend until smooth.

4. Put the paste from the blender into a large bowl and stir in the melted butter and raisins until a runny batter forms.

5. The linseed that has been soaking in water should have formed a thick gel. Pour all of this into the batter and stir well.

6. Sift the flour and baking powder into the batter and mix to combine. If the batter is too thick, add a little coconut milk until you have a pouring consistency.

7. Pour the batter into the prepared loaf tin and bake in the centre of the oven for 30–40 minutes or until golden brown.

8. Turn the loaf out of the tin onto a wire rack to cool. For best results, wait until the loaf is totally cool before slicing.

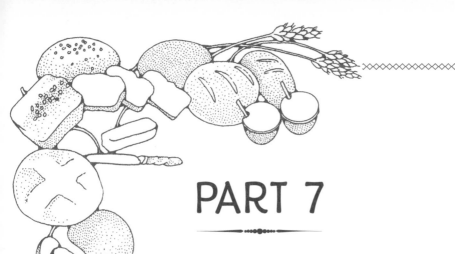

PART 7

QUICK & SWEET BREADS

*The name 'quick bread' says it all – a bread
that can be made speedily because there
is no waiting around for the leavening
agent to work. In addition to quick breads,
this section also includes recipes for sweet
breads that may require the use of
yeast to help them rise.*

COOKING QUICK BREADS

Pure quick breads need no yeast; instead another type of leavening agent, such as baking powder or bicarbonate of soda, gives them their lightness and texture. Quick breads are especially useful when you want to put bread on the table at short notice.

Just as when baking bread with yeast, measure out all the ingredients for quick breads exactly. Don't be tempted to add more baking powder than is given in the recipe, thinking that this will make the bread rise more – all you will achieve is an unpleasant taste on your tongue.

Quick breads don't require the kneading time of ordinary bread. In fact, when you add your raising agent (baking powder or bicarbonate of soda), try to work the batter as little as possible – otherwise the flour's natural gluten will start working and this might result in a tough crumb.

If you are not using a fan oven, try to bake in the centre of the oven, as the heat is often much higher at the top and lower at the bottom of the oven. If you do find the top of your loaf is browning too quickly, protect it with a sheet of kitchen foil.

If the recipe calls for plain flour and baking powder, don't be tempted to substitute self-raising flour (which already has baking powder added). Because you cannot assess exactly how much baking powder is present in the flour, you may not get the quantities exact.

Unlike yeast breads, which are turned out of the tin as soon as they are cooked, quick breads are left in their tin for about 10 minutes before cooling on a wire rack.

Quick breads freeze well. After thawing them at room temperature, reheat at 200°C/400°F/gas mark 6 before serving.

LEMON & LAVENDER BREAD

Make this bread when lavender is in bloom and top it with slices of fresh strawberries or raspberries.

INGREDIENTS *Makes 2 loaves*
325g/11oz plain flour
1½ tsp bicarbonate of soda
1 tsp baking powder
¾ tsp salt
115g/4oz unsalted butter, softened
300g/10oz caster sugar
3 eggs
350g/12oz avocado flesh, mashed
2 tbsp lemon juice
175ml/6fl oz milk
2 tbsp fresh lavender, finely
   chopped
1 tbsp grated lemon zest

METHOD
1. Preheat the oven to 180°C/ 350°C/gas mark 4. Grease and lightly flour two 450g/1lb loaf tins.
2. Sift the flour, bicarbonate of soda, baking powder and salt into a bowl and put to one side.
3. In another bowl, cream together the butter and sugar until light and fluffy. Add the eggs one at a time, beating them well into the mixture. Beat in the avocado flesh and lemon juice with the last egg.
4. Pour the egg mixture into the flour, alternating it with the milk. Fold gently until everything is mixed together. Gently fold in the lavender and lemon zest, mixing only enough to combine them evenly and thus avoid knocking too much air out of the mixture.
5. Pour the mixture into the prepared tins and bake in the preheated oven for about 1 hour, or until a skewer inserted in the centre comes out clean.
6. Leave the bread to cool in the tin for 10 minutes before turning it out onto a wire rack to cool completely.

DATE LOAF

Treacle gives this bread its lovely dark colour. If you enjoy a mix of sweet and savoury, try a slice with some mature stilton.

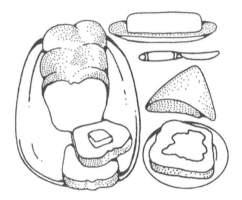

INGREDIENTS *Makes 1 loaf*
3½ tsp dried yeast
300ml/10fl oz warm water
225g/8oz strong white bread flour
225g/8oz wholemeal flour
1 tsp sea salt
60g/2oz butter, softened
   and diced
1 tbsp treacle
115g/4oz dried dates, chopped

METHOD
1. Dissolve the yeast in 2 tablespoons of the warm water and leave to stand for 10 minutes until the mixture is frothy on top.
2. Sift the flours and salt into a large bowl; any grains left in the sieve should be tipped in as well. Rub in the butter with your fingertips until the mixture resembles breadcrumbs.
3. Make a well in the flour and pour in the yeast mixture, treacle and enough of the remaining water to form a soft dough.
4. Turn the dough out onto a lightly floured surface and

knead for 10–15 minutes until it is smooth and elastic in texture. Place the dough in a lightly oiled bowl, cover with a damp tea towel and leave to rise for 1 hour or until it has doubled in size.

5. Knock back the dough, then knead it for a further 2–3 minutes. Press the dates into the top of the dough and chafe until they are fully incorporated. Shape the dough into a round and dust it with flour. Make diagonal lines on the surface with a sharp knife to form several diamonds. Place the loaf on a greased baking tray, lightly dusted with flour. Cover it with a damp tea towel and leave to prove for 30 minutes or until it has doubled in size.

6. Preheat the oven to 220°C/425°F/gas mark 7.

7. Bake the loaf in the centre of the oven for 30–35 minutes or until it is golden and sounds hollow when tapped on the base.

8. Remove from the oven and leave to cool on a wire rack before slicing.

NO-YEAST VERSION

225g/8oz dried dates, chopped
175ml/6fl oz boiling water
2 tsp baking soda
150g/5½oz brown sugar
60g/2oz butter
1 tsp vanilla essence
1 large egg
200g/7oz white flour
½ tsp salt

Preheat the oven to 180°C/350°F/gas mark 4. Soak the dates in the boiling water for 5 minutes. Add the baking soda, sugar, butter, vanilla, egg, flour and salt and beat well until you have a smooth mixture. Spoon the mixture into a greased loaf tin and bake for 40–50 minutes or until a skewer comes out clean when inserted in the middle of the loaf. Cool on a wire rack.

BARA BRITH

This traditional Welsh fruit bread or 'speckled bread' can be made with yeast or self-raising flour, as in this recipe.

INGREDIENTS *Makes 2 large loaves*
2 tea bags
330ml/11fl oz boiling water
675g/1½lb dried mixed fruit
175g/6oz light brown muscovado
    sugar
400ml/14fl oz milk
150g/5½oz butter, diced
60g/2oz glacé cherries, chopped
325g/11oz self-raising flour
1 tsp bicarbonate of soda
1 tsp ground mixed spice
3 large eggs, beaten

METHOD
1. Put the tea bags in a heatproof jug and pour the boiling water over them. Stir and leave to infuse for 3–4 minutes.
2. Put the dried fruit in a bowl, squeeze out the tea bags and pour the tea over the fruit. Cover and soak for at least 5 hours.
3. Line two 900g/2lb loaf tins with baking parchment. Preheat the oven to 180°C/350°F/gas mark 4. Drain the soaked fruit.
4. Put the sugar, milk, butter, mixed fruit and cherries in a saucepan and simmer for 4 minutes. Pour into a bowl and leave to cool.
5. When the mixture has cooled, sift the flour, bicarbonate of soda and mixed spice into the fruit mixture and stir to combine. Add the beaten eggs and mix well.
6. Divide the mixture evenly between the two loaf tins. Place them side-by-side in the centre of the oven and bake for about 1 hour. Test with a skewer to see whether the loaves are cooked; if it comes out clean, they are ready.
7. Leave the loaves to cool in the tins. You can freeze one loaf to eat later, if you wish.

SAVOURY SCONES

This is an easy scone recipe and a good way of introducing children to the fun of bread making. The scones don't need time to rise, so children won't get bored waiting for a result.

INGREDIENTS *Makes 8 scones*
225g/8oz plain flour
½ tsp fine sea salt
1 tsp bicarbonate of soda
2 tsp cream of tartar
60g/2oz unsalted butter, chilled
    and diced
85g/3oz mature cheddar, grated
½ tsp English mustard powder
½ tsp cayenne pepper
150ml/5fl oz milk, plus a little
    extra for glazing

METHOD
1. Preheat the oven to 220°C/425°F/gas mark 7. Lightly grease a baking tray and dust with flour.
2. Sift the flour, salt, bicarbonate of soda and cream of tartar into a large bowl. Add the diced butter and work it into the flour with your fingertips until you have fine breadcrumbs. Mix in the cheese, mustard powder and cayenne pepper and make a well in the centre of the mixture.
3. Gradually add the milk to the well, stirring with the blade of a table knife until you have a soft dough.
4. Put the dough onto a lightly floured surface and form into a ball. Roll the dough out until it is about 2.5cm/1in thick and then cut out 8 circles measuring 5cm/2in in diameter.
5. Place the scones on the prepared baking tray and brush with a little milk.
6. Bake in the centre of the preheated oven for 8–10 minutes or until the scones are risen and golden brown in colour.
7. Cool them a little on a wire rack before splitting them and serving with butter.

LUXURY FRUIT SCONES

For a luxury version of the English scone, try a recipe with cream incorporated into the dough. You can still have clotted cream and jam with these scones as well – they are for sheer indulgence!

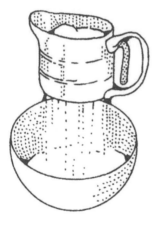

INGREDIENTS *Makes 12 scones*
600g/1lb 5oz plain flour
150g/5½oz butter, chilled
   and diced
150g/5½oz caster sugar
40g/1¼oz baking powder
280g/10oz sultanas
190ml/6½fl oz double cream
190ml/6½fl oz milk
1 egg, beaten with a pinch of
   salt, to glaze

METHOD
1. Preheat the oven to 220°C/ 425°F/gas mark 7.
2. Sift the flour into a large mixing bowl and add the diced butter. Work it in with your fingertips until the mixture has the consistency of breadcrumbs.
3. Add the sugar and baking powder and mix well. Add the sultanas and mix until they are evenly distributed throughout the flour mixture.
4. Add the cream and milk and mix until all the ingredients are combined and start to form a dough.
5. Turn out the dough onto a lightly floured work surface. Press down on the dough, then fold it in half. Press down again and fold in the opposite direction.

Repeat until you have a roughly square shape. Dust the top and bottom of the dough with flour, cover with a tea towel and leave to rest for 15 minutes.

6. Roll out the dough on a lightly floured surface until it is about 3cm/1¼in thick. Brush off any excess flour and then cut out 12 circles about 6cm/2½in in diameter. Roll out the scraps and cut more scones until you have used up all the dough.

7. Lay the scones on baking trays, making sure they are not too close together.

8. Glaze the top of the scones with the egg wash. Leave them to rest for 2 minutes then glaze again.

9. Turn down the heat in the preheated oven to 200°C/400°F/ gas mark 6. Bake the scones for about 20 minutes or until they are well risen. The tops and bottoms should be a light golden brown.

10. Turn the scones out onto a wire rack to cool a little and eat as soon as possible with clotted cream, jam and a steaming cup of tea.

BRIOCHE

Brioche is a light, buttery, sweet bread from France. It is usually eaten at breakfast but makes a delicious snack any time of day.

INGREDIENTS *Makes 12 brioches*
250g/9oz strong white bread flour
½ tsp salt
2 tbsp caster sugar
1 sachet easy-blend yeast
3 large eggs, beaten
5 tbsp warm milk
1 tsp vanilla essence
115g/4oz unsalted butter, softened
   and diced
1 egg, beaten, to glaze

METHOD
1. Sift the flour and salt into a large bowl. Add the sugar and yeast, then make a well in the centre. Add the beaten eggs, milk and vanilla to the flour and stir until a soft dough forms.
2. Turn the dough out onto a lightly floured surface and knead for 5 minutes.
3. Add the butter a few pieces at a time, making sure it is fully worked into the dough before adding the next pieces.
4. Once you have worked in all the butter, wrap the dough in cling film and leave in the fridge for at least 1 hour. You can make the dough in advance if you like and leave it overnight.
5. Grease 12 small brioche tins. Knock back the dough and knead for 2–3 minutes on a lightly floured surface. Divide the dough into 12 pieces and shape each into a ball. Put into the brioche tins, cover with a tea towel and leave in a warm place for about 20 minutes or until doubled in size.
6. Preheat the oven to 200°C/400°F/gas mark 6.
7. Brush the tops of the brioches with beaten egg and bake for 12–15 minutes, or until golden brown. Turn out of the tin and cool on a wire rack before slicing.

CARROT & RAISIN MUFFINS

These make a delightful breakfast served warm with some fresh fruit and a steaming cup of coffee or tea.

INGREDIENTS *Makes 8 muffins*
200g/7oz self-raising flour
¼ tsp salt
½ tsp ground cinnamon
75g/2½oz sugar
120ml/4fl oz milk
50g/1¾oz butter
175g/6oz carrot, grated
115g/4oz raisins
1 egg, beaten

FOR THE CREAM CHEESE TOPPING:
225g/8oz cream cheese
50g/1¾oz butter, softened
50g/1¾oz light brown sugar
few drops of vanilla essence

METHOD

1. Preheat the oven to 200°C/400°F/gas mark 6. Prepare your muffin tin by lining it with paper cases; set aside.

2. Sift the flour, salt and cinnamon into a bowl and stir in the sugar.

3. Put the milk and butter into a saucepan and heat gently until the butter has melted. Set aside to cool slightly.

4. Mix the carrots and raisins into the flour mixture and make a well in the centre. Add the beaten egg and milk mixture from the saucepan and stir until you have a smooth consistency and all the ingredients are combined.

5. Spoon the mixture into the paper muffin cases, put the muffin tin in the oven and bake for 15 minutes until the muffins are firm to the touch and golden in colour.

6. Leave to cool on a wire rack. Meanwhile, make the cream cheese topping by beating the four ingredients together until light and fluffy. Spread some on each muffin when they are cool.

HOT CROSS BUNS

Although hot cross buns are traditionally eaten at Easter, they are
simply too delicious not to be enjoyed the rest of the year.

INGREDIENTS *Makes 12 buns*
2½ tsp dried yeast
250ml/8fl oz warm milk
450g/1lb strong white bread flour
1 tsp salt
85g/3oz unsalted butter, softened
    and diced
85g/3oz soft light brown sugar
1 tsp mixed spice
¼ tsp freshly grated nutmeg
½ tsp ground cinnamon
1 large egg, beaten
115g/4oz raisins
85g/3oz sultanas
60g/2oz candied lemon peel,
    finely chopped

FOR THE CROSSES:
100ml/3½fl oz water
100g/3½oz plain flour
1 medium egg

FOR THE GLAZE:
2 tbsp golden syrup

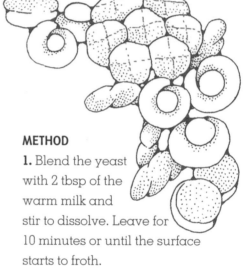

METHOD
1. Blend the yeast
with 2 tbsp of the
warm milk and
stir to dissolve. Leave for
10 minutes or until the surface
starts to froth.
2. Sift the flour and salt into a
large bowl. Add the diced butter
and work it into the flour with
your fingertips until the mixture
resembles fine breadcrumbs.
Stir in the sugar and spices and
make a well in the centre.
3. Add the yeast to the flour
mixture together with the
egg and enough of the

remaining milk to form a soft, smooth dough.

4. Turn the dough out onto a lightly floured surface and knead for 5 minutes until it is smooth and elastic in texture. Gradually incorporate the raisins, sultanas and candied peel by chafing the dough.

5. Put the dough in a lightly oiled bowl, cover with a damp tea towel and leave to rise for 1 hour in a warm place or until it has doubled in size.

6. Knock back the dough, then knead it for 2–3 minutes on a lightly floured surface.

7. Cut the dough into 12 equal pieces and shape them into balls with your hands. Place on a greased baking tray with plenty of space between each one to give them room to double in size. Cover with a damp tea towel and leave to prove for another hour.

8. Preheat the oven to 200°C/400°F/gas mark 6.

9. To form the crosses, make a paste out of the water, flour and egg. Pour the paste into a icing bag with a plain nozzle and pipe a cross on the surface of each bun.

10. Place the tray of buns in the preheated oven and bake for 15 minutes or until they are golden brown.

11. Remove the buns from the oven and while they are still warm brush them with slightly warmed golden syrup. Leave them to cool on a wire rack and serve them split and buttered.

VARIATION

Substitute 115g/4oz of cocoa powder for the same amount of flour and replace the preserved fruit with 250g/9oz chocolate chips to make a wonderful chocolate version of these buns.

CHELSEA BUNS

The Chelsea bun, with its traditional spiral shape, originated in the 18th century at the Bun House, Chelsea.

INGREDIENTS *Makes 10 buns*
450g/1lb strong white bread flour
1 tsp salt
1 sachet easy-blend yeast
300ml/10fl oz milk
40g/1¼oz butter, softened
1 medium egg, beaten
vegetable oil, for greasing

FOR THE FILLING:
30g/1oz unsalted butter, melted
85g/3oz soft brown sugar
2 tsp ground cinnamon
150g/5½oz raisins

FOR THE GLAZE:
2 tbsp caster sugar
2 tbsp milk

METHOD

1. Sift the flour, salt and yeast into a large bowl and make a well in the centre.

2. Warm the milk and butter in a saucepan over a gentle heat until the butter has melted and the liquid is at 37°C/98.6°F.

3. Add the milk mixture and beaten egg to the flour and mix until the ingredients form a soft dough. If it is too sticky, add a little extra flour.

4. Turn the dough out onto a floured surface and knead for 5 minutes until the dough is smooth and elastic in texture and no longer feels sticky.

5. Place the dough in a lightly oiled bowl and turn until it is covered in the oil. Cover the bowl with a damp tea towel and leave in a warm place to rise for 1 hour, or until the dough has doubled in size.

6. Lightly grease a baking tray.

7. Knock back the dough to its original size and turn it out onto a lightly floured surface. Dust

a rolling pin with flour and roll out the dough into a rectangle approximately 5mm/¼in thick.

8. Brush the surface of the dough with the melted butter using a soft-bristled pastry brush. Sprinkle the brown sugar evenly over the surface of the dough, followed by the cinnamon and the raisins.

9. Starting at one end, roll the dough up into a tight cylinder and seal the final edge using the prongs of a fork.

10. Using a sharp knife, cut the cylinder into ten 4cm/1½in slices and place them on the greased baking tray, leaving enough room between each one for them to spread.Cover with a damp tea towel and put in a warm place to rise for 30 minutes.

11. Preheat the oven to 190°C/ 375°F/gas mark 5.

12. Bake the buns in the preheated oven for 20–25 minutes, or until they have risen and are golden brown.

13. While the buns are cooking, make the glaze by heating the sugar and milk in a saucepan until it comes to a rolling boil. Reduce the heat and simmer gently for 2–3 minutes.

14. When the buns are cooked, remove them from the oven and brush them immediately with the milk/sugar glaze. Leave them to cool on a wire rack before serving.

WAFFLES

You need a waffle iron to make these light, crisp and delicious waffles, which are always a hit with children for breakfast.

INGREDIENTS *Makes 4 waffles*
250g/9oz plain flour
1 tsp baking powder
¼ tsp salt
2 eggs, separated
240ml/8fl oz milk
120ml/4fl oz vegetable oil

METHOD
1. Sift the flour, baking powder and salt into a medium-sized mixing bowl and make a well in the centre.
2. In a separate bowl, beat the egg yolks and stir in the milk and oil.
3. Add the egg and milk mixture to the dry ingredients. Stir only until the ingredients have just mixed – the batter should be still lumpy at this stage.
4. In another bowl, beat the egg whites until they form stiff peaks.
5. Gently fold the egg whites into the batter – take care not to overwork the mixture at this stage as you do not want to knock the air out of the egg whites.
6. Spoon the batter into your waffle iron. Make sure you do not overfill it or it will spill out over the sides. Cook according to the manufacturer's instructions.
7. Serve the hot waffles with some knobs of butter and real maple syrup (or chocolate sauce) and banana for an indulgent breakfast treat.

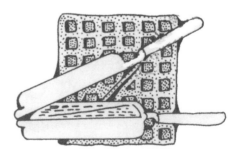

STICKY MALT LOAF

This sticky, fruited malt loaf is incredibly easy to make. It is dark in colour because the fruit is soaked in tea.

INGREDIENTS *Makes 2 loaves*
150ml/5fl oz hot black tea
175g/6oz malt extract, plus extra
    for glazing
85g/3oz dark muscovado sugar
300g/10oz mixed sultanas, raisins
    and chopped dates
2 large eggs, beaten
250g/9oz plain flour
1 tsp baking powder
½ tsp bicarbonate of soda

METHOD
1. Preheat the oven to 150°C/
300°F/gas mark 2.
2. Grease two 450g/1lb loaf tins
with butter and line them with
baking parchment.
3. Pour the hot tea into a large
mixing bowl and add the malt,
sugar, dried fruit and chopped
dates. Stir well, then add the
beaten eggs.
4. Sift the flour, baking powder
and bicarbonate of soda into
the tea mixture then stir quickly
to combine.
5. Pour the mixture into the
prepared tins and bake in the
oven for 50 minutes or until firm
and well risen.
6. Remove the loaves from the
tins and place on a wire rack to
cool. While they are still warm,
brush the tops with a little
warmed malt extract. If you have
the willpower to leave them
for 2–3 days before eating, the
loaves will become even stickier.
They will keep well if wrapped in
baking parchment and stored in
an airtight container.
7. If you wish to freeze the second
loaf, wrap it in baking parchment
and then in kitchen foil. It will
keep for up to 4 months in the
freezer. To thaw, leave it at room
temperature for 5 hours.

LARDY CAKE

Also known as lardy bread, this is a traditional richly spiced bread made by layering thinly rolled dough with spicy fruit.

INGREDIENTS *Makes 1 large loaf*

FOR THE DOUGH:

3½ tsp dried yeast

300ml/10fl oz warm water

450g/1lb strong white bread flour

1 tsp salt

30g/1oz golden caster sugar

15g/½oz lard, softened and diced

FOR THE FILLING:

85g/3oz lard, diced

85g/3oz soft light brown sugar

115g/4oz raisins

115g/4oz sultanas

30g/1oz candied lemon peel, chopped

1 tsp mixed spice

FOR THE GLAZE:

2 tsp sunflower oil

2 tbsp caster sugar

METHOD

1. Dissolve the yeast in 2 tablespoons of the warm water and leave for 10 minutes until a froth forms on the surface.

2. Sift the flour and salt into a large bowl, add the sugar and rub in the lard with your fingertips until the mixture resembles breadcrumbs. Make a well in the centre.

3. Pour the yeast mixture into the well in the flour and gradually add the remaining water. Mix with your hands until you have a smooth dough.

4. Turn the dough out onto a lightly floured surface and knead for 10 minutes until it becomes smooth and elastic in texture. Place the dough in a lightly oiled bowl, cover with a damp tea towel and leave to rise for 1 hour or until it has doubled in size.

5. Knock back the dough then turn it out onto a lightly floured surface and knead for a further 2–3 minutes. Lightly dust a rolling pin with flour and then roll the dough out into a rectangle until it is approximately 5mm/¼in thick.

6. Using half the amount of lard for the filling, cover the top two-thirds of the surface with dots of lard. Sprinkle over half the sugar, half the dried fruits and peel and half the mixed spice, leaving the bottom third empty and about 4cm/1½in clear on all other sides.

7. Fold the dough in three, folding the bottom third up and the top third down, sealing the edges by pressing them with a rolling pin. Turn the dough a quarter turn (90 degrees), roll lightly into another rectangle and cover with the remaining ingredients and fold as above.

8. Grease a 25cm × 20cm/10in × 8in Swiss roll tin. Roughly shape the dough so that it will fit inside the prepared tin. Place the dough inside the tin, flatten it with your hands so that it fits snugly, cover with a damp tea towel and leave to prove in a warm place

for 30–40 minutes or until it has doubled in size.

9. Preheat the oven to 200°C/400°F/gas mark 6.

10. Brush the dough with the oil and sprinkle with sugar. Using a sharp knife, mark a diamond pattern on top.

11. Bake in the preheated oven for 30–40 minutes until golden brown. Remove from the oven and leave the cake to cool in the tin before serving.

NEED TO KNOW

The filling and folding stages of the lardy cake can be rather messy as the filling tries to break out of any weak parts in the dough. Don't worry too much –patch it up as best you can by poking the filling back in and continue with the folding and rolling.

DUTCH APPLE BREAD

This is a delicious fruity, streusel-topped bread that freezes
exceptionally well. It is a great way to use up windfall apples.

INGREDIENTS *Makes 1 loaf*

FOR THE DOUGH:

115g/4oz butter, softened

225g/8oz sugar

2 eggs

1 tsp vanilla essence

115g/4oz plain flour

1 tsp baking soda

½ tsp salt

90ml/3fl oz buttermilk

1 large apple, peeled, cored
   and chopped

45g/1½oz walnuts, finely chopped

FOR THE STREUSEL:

60g/2oz plain flour

2 tbsp golden granulated sugar

2 tbsp soft brown sugar

1 tsp ground cinnamon

45g/1½oz butter, softened

METHOD

1. Preheat the oven to 180°C/
350°F/gas mark 4. Grease a
450g/1lb loaf tin.

2. Cream the butter and sugar
together in a large mixing bowl.
Beat in the eggs one at a time,
adding the vanilla essence with
the second egg.

3. Sift the flour, baking soda and
salt into the creamed mixture.
Gradually add the buttermilk
and mix until combined. Gently
fold in the apple and nuts.

4. Pour the mixture into the
prepared tin. Now make the
streusel by mixing the flour,
sugars and cinnamon. Cut in the
butter until the mixture resembles
breadcrumbs. Sprinkle evenly
over the top of the bread.

5. Bake in the preheated oven for
55–60 minutes or until a skewer
inserted into the bread comes
out clean. Cool in the tin for 10
minutes before turning out on to
a wire rack to cool completely.

CHOCOLATE CHIP MUFFINS

This is a traditional recipe for chocolate chip muffins. These are different from English muffins, which have a yeast-based dough.

INGREDIENTS *Makes 6 muffins*
250g/9oz plain flour
125g/4½oz caster sugar
1 tsp baking powder
1 tsp bicarbonate of soda
3 tbsp vegetable oil
1 egg
150ml/5fl oz semi-skimmed milk
1 tsp vanilla essence
100g/3½oz dark chocolate chips

METHOD
1. Preheat the oven to 220°C/425°F/gas mark 7. Prepare your muffin tin by lining it with paper cases and set aside.
2. In a bowl, combine the plain flour, sugar, baking powder and bicarbonate of soda and set aside.
3. In another bowl, combine the oil, egg, milk and vanilla essence and mix well.
4. Sift all the dry ingredients from the first bowl into the liquid, making sure that you hold the sieve high to incorporate as much air as possible. Add the chocolate chips and fold the mixture 15 times only.
5. Spoon the mixture into the muffin cases so they are three-quarters full and place the tin on the middle shelf of your oven. Reduce the temperature to 180°C/350°F/gas mark 4 and bake for 25–30 minutes or until the tops of the muffins are firm to the touch.
6. Leave the muffins in the tin for 2 minutes after you have taken them out of the oven, before placing on a wire rack to cool.

If you want your chocolate chips to hold their shape inside the muffins, put them in the freezer for 30 minutes before using.

GINGERBREAD

Instead of making one large loaf, try baking gingerbread as individual cakes for a teatime treat.

INGREDIENTS *Makes 12*

115g/4oz plain white flour
1½ tsp ground ginger
1½ tsp ground cinnamon
1 tsp bicarbonate of soda
115g/4oz soft brown sugar
60g/2oz stem ginger, finely
   chopped
115g/4oz unsalted butter
115g/4oz black treacle
1 large egg, beaten
150ml/5fl oz milk

METHOD

1. Preheat the oven to 180°C/
350°F/gas mark 4.
2. Line a 12-hole muffin tin with
paper cases.
3. Sift all the dry ingredients in a
large bowl and mix thoroughly.

Make a well in the centre.
4. Gently heat the butter and
treacle together in a small
saucepan until the butter has
melted. Remove from the heat
and stir in the beaten egg and
the milk.
5. Pour into the flour mixture and
mix well to incorporate all the
ingredients.
6. Pour the mixture into the muffin
cases and bake in the centre of
the preheated oven for 15–20
minutes, until the gingerbread
has risen and is a rich brown
in colour.
7. Take the paper cases out of
the muffin tin and leave the
gingerbread to cool on a
wire rack.

BANANA & COURGETTE BREAD

This is a delicious moist bread with a strong banana flavour and the unusual addition of grated courgette.

INGREDIENTS *Makes 1 loaf*
250g/9oz plain flour
1 tsp bicarbonate of soda
½ tsp salt
115g/4oz butter, softened
175g/6oz caster sugar
2 eggs, beaten
450g/1lb ripe bananas, mashed
1 medium courgette, grated

METHOD
1. Preheat the oven to 180°C/350°F/gas mark 4. Lightly grease a 450g/1lb loaf tin.
2. Sift the flour, bicarbonate of soda and salt into a large bowl.
3. In another bowl, cream together the butter and sugar until light and fluffy.
4. Add the beaten eggs, mashed bananas and grated courgette to the butter mixture and stir until thoroughly combined.
5. Add the banana mixture to the flour in the other bowl, folding gently until the ingredients are fully incorporated. Pour the mixture into the prepared loaf tin.
6. Bake in the preheated oven for 50–65 minutes or until a skewer inserted in the centre of the loaf comes out clean.
7. Leave the bread to cool in the tin for 10 minutes before turning it out onto a wire rack.

VARIATIONS

There are many things you can add to banana bread – try substituting 140g/5oz carrot or dark chocolate chips for the courgette.

DOUGHNUTS

This is a very simple recipe for doughnuts. Children will enjoy making them, as they can fill each one with jam before tucking in.

INGREDIENTS *Makes 8–10*
3½ tsp dried yeast
150ml/5fl oz warm water
250g/9oz strong white bread flour
30g/1oz unsalted butter, softened
    and diced
40g/1¼oz caster sugar
sunflower oil, for deep frying
350g/12oz raspberry jam (or
    flavour of choice)
caster sugar mixed with a little
    ground cinnamon, for dusting

METHOD
1. Dissolve the yeast in 2 tablespoons of the warm water and set aside for 10 minutes or until the top has turned frothy.
2. Sift the flour into a large bowl and add the diced butter. Work this into the flour with your fingertips until the mixture resembles breadcrumbs. Stir in 40g/1¼oz of the caster sugar and make a well in the centre.
3. Add the yeast liquid and enough of the remaining water to the flour mixture and mix with your hands until a soft, smooth dough forms.
4. Turn the dough out onto a lightly floured surface and knead

for 10–15 minutes, or until it is smooth and elastic in texture.

5. Place the dough in a lightly oiled bowl, cover with a damp tea towel and leave in a warm place for 1 hour or until the dough has doubled in size.

6. Knock back the dough and knead it for another 2–3 minutes on a lightly floured surface.

7. Divide the dough into 8–10 pieces, depending on how large you like your doughnuts. Shape each piece into a ball with your hands. Place the balls on a lightly floured board, cover with a damp tea towel and leave to prove for 30 minutes.

8. Towards the end of the proving time, heat the oil to 170°C/338°F in a deep, heavy-based pan. Fry the dough balls in batches for 5–10 minutes or until they are golden brown.

9. Remove them with a slotted spoon and allow to drain on kitchen paper.

10. To make the jam easier to work with, warm it slightly in a small saucepan but do not allow it to get too hot. Put the warm jam into a piping bag with a small nozzle. Push the nozzle into the side of each doughnut and pipe a little jam into each one.

11. Mix the caster sugar and a little ground cinnamon together in a bowl and then roll each warm doughnut in the sugar mixture until thoroughly coated.

12. Leave the doughnuts to cool on a wire rack before eating.

VARIATIONS

Try making some doughnut rings by flattening the balls with the palm of your hand and cutting a small circle out of the middle with a biscuit cutter. Ice the cooked doughnuts by mixing together 115g/4oz icing sugar with sufficient cold water to make a runny consistency.

PUMPKIN BREAD

Next time you are making a Hallowe'en lantern for your children, don't waste the pumpkin flesh – bake this delicious loaf.

INGREDIENTS *Makes 1 large loaf*
450g/1lb pumpkin flesh
175g/6oz soft brown sugar
115g/4oz butter, softened
3 eggs, beaten
225g/8oz plain flour
2 tsp baking powder
1 tsp ground cinnamon
½ tsp salt
½ tsp ground nutmeg
225g/8oz dark chocolate chips

METHOD

1. Cut the pumpkin flesh into small pieces and steam until soft. Transfer to a food processor and whizz until you have a fine purée.

2. Preheat the oven to 180°C/ 350°F/gas mark 4. Grease a 900g/2lb loaf tin.

3. Combine the puréed pumpkin, brown sugar, butter and eggs until you have a creamy mixture.

4. In a separate bowl, sift the flour, baking powder, cinnamon, salt and nutmeg. Gradually add this to the pumpkin mixture until you have a moist but thick consistency. You should be able to stand a spoon in the mix without it falling over.

5. Add the chocolate chips and mix until evenly distributed.

6. Spoon the mixture into the prepared loaf tin, place in the centre of the oven and bake for about 1 hour or until a skewer inserted in the middle comes out clean.

7. Leave to cool in the tin for 10 minutes before turning out onto a wire rack to cool completely before serving.

This recipe also works well with chopped walnuts instead of chocolate chips.

TEA CAKES

Spicy tea cakes packed full of fruit, split in half and toasted with plenty of butter are the epitome of English tea.

INGREDIENTS *Makes 10*
450g/1lb strong white bread flour
1 tsp salt
60g/2oz unsalted butter, diced
1 sachet easy-blend yeast
30g/1oz caster sugar
85g/3oz raisins
85g/3oz sultanas
½ tsp cinnamon
300ml/10fl oz warm semi-
    skimmed milk, plus extra
    for brushing

METHOD

1. Sift the flour and salt into a large bowl. Rub in the butter with your fingertips until the mixture is the consistency of fine breadcrumbs.

2. Add the yeast, sugar, raisins, sultanas and cinnamon, mix and make a well in the centre.

3. Gradually add the warm milk until you have a smooth, soft dough. Add a little more milk if your mixture is too dry.

4. Turn the dough out onto a lightly floured surface and knead for about 10 minutes or until smooth and elastic in texture. Place the dough in a lightly oiled bowl, cover with a damp tea towel and leave to rise in a warm place for 1 hour or until doubled in size.

5. Knock back the dough to its original size and knead for 2–3 minutes on a lightly floured surface. Divide it into 10 pieces and shape into round tea cakes.

6. Put the tea cakes on 2 greased baking trays, cover with a damp tea towel and leave to rise for 1 hour or until puffy.

7. Preheat the oven to 220°C/425°F/gas mark 7. Brush the tops of the tea cakes with milk and bake for 10–15 minutes in the centre of the oven or until browned.

PRUNE & CHOCOLATE BREAD

Try this amazing combination of prunes and chocolate – it gives the bread a decadent rich, sweet flavour.

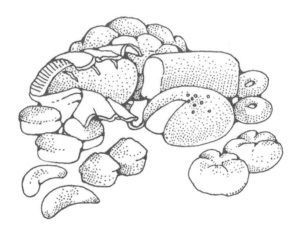

INGREDIENTS *Makes 2 oval loaves*
2½ tsp dried yeast
450ml/15fl oz warm water
375g/13oz strong white bread
   flour
375g/13oz wholemeal flour
2 tsp salt
350g/12oz pitted prunes, chopped
350g/12oz dark chocolate,
   chopped
20g/¾oz unsalted butter, diced
1 large egg, beaten

METHOD
1. Dissolve the yeast in 2 tbsp of warm water and leave for 10 minutes until a froth forms on the surface.
2. Sift the flours and salt into a large bowl, tipping any grains left in the sieve into the bowl. Make a well in the centre.
3. Add the yeast mixture and gradually add three quarters of the remaining water until

the dough is firm and starting to leave the sides of the bowl. If the dough is too stiff, add the remaining water.

4. Turn the dough out onto a lightly floured surface and knead well for 10 minutes until it has a smooth and elastic texture. Place the dough in a lightly oiled bowl, cover with a damp tea towel and leave to rise in a warm place for 1 hour or until doubled in size.

5. Knock back the dough, turn it onto a lightly floured surface and knead for a further 2–3 minutes.

6. Press the dough with the palm of your hand until a well is formed and then push the chopped prunes, chocolate, diced butter and beaten egg into the middle. Fold the edges into the middle and chafe the dough until all the ingredients are evenly distributed. If the dough gets too sticky at this stage, add a little more flour, but be careful not to add too much.

7. Preheat the oven to 220°C/ 425°F/gas mark 7. Grease 2 baking trays.

8. Divide the dough in half and form it into two ovals. With a sharp knife, make three diagonal cuts in the top of each loaf and place the dough on the prepared baking trays. Cover the loaves with a damp tea towel and leave to prove in a warm place for 10 minutes.

9. Bake the loaves for 20–25 minutes or until they are golden brown and sound hollow when tapped on the base.

10. Leave them to cool on a wire rack and serve while they are still warm.

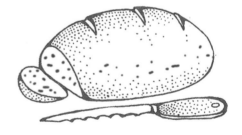

This bread will keep for 2 days in an airtight container, after which it makes really good toast.

PANETTONE

This round fruit cake comes from Italy and is traditionally eaten at Christmas and Easter. It is usually baked in a special mould which gives it a round, deep shape. This version is baked in a regular round cake tin and still tastes just as good.

INGREDIENTS *Makes 1 large loaf*
1 sachet easy-blend yeast
240ml/8fl oz warm water
50g/1¾oz sugar
2 eggs, beaten
120ml/4fl oz natural yogurt
2 tsp vanilla essence
10g/¼oz lemon zest, grated
1 tsp salt
450g/1lb unbleached bread flour
60g/2oz currants
60g/2oz raisins
1 tbsp icing sugar
15g/½oz unsalted butter, melted

METHOD

1. In a medium-sized bowl, combine the yeast, water and sugar. Cover and leave to stand for 10 minutes or until a foam has formed on the surface.

2. Add the beaten eggs, yogurt, vanilla essence, lemon zest and salt and mix well to combine.

3. Stir in the flour a spoonful at a time until the dough starts to form a soft, workable ball and comes away from the sides of the bowl.

4. Turn the dough out onto a lightly floured surface and knead for 10 minutes until it is soft and elastic, but not sticky. If you think the dough is too sticky, add a little more flour at this stage.

5. Place the dough in a lightly oiled bowl, cover with a damp tea towel and leave in a warm place to rise for 1 hour, or until it has doubled in size.

6. Preheat the oven to 180°C/350°F/gas mark 4. Grease a round 20cm/8in cake tin.

7. Put the currants and raisins in a small bowl and dust them with the icing sugar until they are totally coated.

8. Knock back the dough, transfer to a lightly floured surface and chafe in the fruit until it is evenly distributed.

9. Form the dough into a ball and place it in the prepared cake tin. Cover loosely with a tea towel and leave to rise in a warm place for 30 minutes. The dough should rise above the sides of the cake tin when it is ready.

10. Once it has risen, brush the surface with melted butter.

11. Bake in the centre of the preheated oven for 45 minutes or until the loaf is golden brown and a skewer inserted in the middle comes out clean.

12. Leave to cool on a wire rack.

A LITTLE BIT OF HISTORY

There is an interesting story about the origin of the panettone loaf, although no one knows how true it is. A 15th-century falconer fell in love with the daughter of a lowly baker called Toni. To win her over, the falconer disguised himself as a baker and invented a rich bread, to which he added raisins and citrus peel. The result was a tremendous success and became known as 'Pan de Toni' (Toni's bread).

STOLLEN

This is a perfect choice for Christmas as it is packed with fruit and marzipan. It also makes an excellent gift.

INGREDIENTS *Makes 1 loaf*
2 tsp dried yeast
175ml/6fl oz warm milk
1 large egg, beaten
75g/2½oz caster sugar
1½ tsp salt
75g/2½oz unsalted butter, softened
350g/12oz strong white bread flour
60g/2oz currants
60g/2oz sultanas
60g/2oz glacé cherries, quartered
175g/6oz mixed citrus peel, diced
200g/7oz marzipan

FOR DECORATION:
30g/1oz icing sugar
1 tsp ground cinnamon
toasted flaked almonds

METHOD
1. Dissolve the yeast in the warm milk in a small bowl and leave to stand for 10 minutes until it is creamy and frothy on top.

2. In a large bowl, mix together the yeast mixture, beaten egg, caster sugar, salt, butter and three-quarters of the flour. Beat well. Add the remaining flour a spoonful at a time, stirring well after each addition. When the dough starts to form and come away from the sides of the bowl, turn it out onto a lightly floured surface.

3. Knead or chafe the currants, sultanas, cherries and mixed peel into the dough. Continue kneading until the dough is smooth – this should take about 8–10 minutes.

4. Place the dough in a lightly oiled bowl and roll to coat it with the oil. Cover with a damp tea towel and leave to rise in a warm place for 1 hour or until the

warm place for 40 minutes or until it has doubled in size.

8. Towards the end of the proving, preheat the oven to 180°C/350°F/gas mark 4.

9. Bake the stollen in the preheated oven for 10 minutes, then reduce the heat to 150°C/300°F/gas mark 2. Bake for a further 30–40 minutes or until the stollen is golden brown.

10. Allow the stollen to cool on a wire rack. When cool, dust the surface with icing sugar mixed with cinnamon and finish with the toasted flaked almonds.

dough has doubled in size.

5. Lightly grease a baking tray.

6. Knock back the dough, turn it out onto a lightly floured surface and shape into a rectangle.

7. Roll the marzipan into a long, thin rope shape and place it in the centre of the dough. Fold the sides of the dough into the middle to cover the marzipan and pinch the seams together to form a seal. Put the loaf, seam-side down, on to the prepared baking tray. Cover it with a damp tea towel and leave to rise in a

A LITTLE BIT OF HISTORY

In the year 1730, the Lord of Saxony demanded that his chef bake an enormous stollen for a celebration banquet. It weighed 1.8 tonnes and was 8.2m/27ft long and 5.5m/18ft wide!

SALLY LUNN

The forerunner of the Bath bun, the Sally Lunn was considered a delicacy in Georgian England for its light and subtle taste.

INGREDIENTS *Makes 1 loaf*
400g/14oz strong white
   bread flour
1½ tsp salt
1 sachet easy-blend yeast
45g/1½oz caster sugar
45g/1½oz unsalted butter,
   softened and diced
120ml4fl oz warm milk
120ml/4fl oz warm water
60g/2oz sultanas
60g/2oz glacé cherries, quartered
1 tsp ground cinnamon
grated zest of 3 oranges
75g/2½oz icing sugar

METHOD
1. Sift the flour and salt into a large bowl. Add the yeast, sugar and butter and work with your fingertips until the mixture resembles fine breadcrumbs. Gradually add the milk and water and work with your hands until you have a smooth dough. Turn the dough out onto a lightly floured surface and knead for 10 minutes until smooth and elastic.
2. Put the dough into a lightly oiled bowl, cover with a damp tea towel and leave to rise for 1 hour or until double in size.
3. Knock back the dough, add the sultanas, cherries, cinnamon and orange zest and chafe until all the ingredients are evenly spread throughout the dough. Mould into a long sausage shape and place on a greased baking tray. Cover with a tea towel and leave to rise for 1 hour.
4. Preheat the oven to 200°C/ 400°F/gas mark 6.
5. Bake for 20 minutes until golden brown. Cool on a wire rack, then drizzle the surface with the icing sugar mixed with a little water. Cut into slices to serve.

LEMON & BLUEBERRY BREAD

With its pairing of fresh blueberries and lemon, this quick bread
has the taste of summer.

INGREDIENTS *Makes 1 loaf*
75g/2½oz unsalted butter, melted
225g/8oz granulated sugar
2 eggs
120ml/4fl oz milk
1 lemon
175g/6oz self-raising flour
½ tsp salt
115g/4oz blueberries

METHOD
1. Preheat the oven to 180°C/
350°F/gas mark 4. Grease a
450g/1lb loaf tin.
2. In a medium-sized bowl,
combine the melted butter,
sugar, eggs and milk and beat
until blended.
3. Finely grate the zest from the
lemon and squeeze out the juice.
Add both zest and juice to the
mixture in the bowl.
4. Sift the flour and salt into the
mixture and gently fold it in until
the ingredients are thoroughly
combined.
5. Fold in the blueberries
until they are evenly spread
throughout the mixture.
6. Pour the mixture into the
prepared loaf tin and bake in the
preheated oven for 1 hour or until
a skewer comes out clean when
inserted in the middle of the loaf.
7. Remove the loaf from the oven
and leave to cool for 15 minutes
in the tin before turning it out
onto a wire rack to cool further.

PEAR AND ALMOND BREAD

Any bread chef would be proud of this loaf with its distinctive pear flavour, enhanced by a drizzle of dark chocolate on the top.

INGREDIENTS *Makes 1 loaf*
3½ tsp dried yeast
300ml/10fl oz warm milk
450g/1lb strong white bread flour
¼ tsp salt
60g/2oz caster sugar
85g/3oz ground almonds
45g/1½oz unsalted butter,
    softened and diced
2 ripe pears, peeled, cored
    and diced
125g/4½oz flaked almonds
75g/2½oz dark chocolate, melted,
    to decorate

METHOD
1. Dissolve the yeast in 2 tablespoons of the warm milk. Leave to stand for 10 minutes or until it becomes creamy and a froth forms on the surface.
2. Combine the flour, salt, sugar and ground almonds in a large bowl. Add the butter and work with your fingertips until the mixture resembles breadcrumbs. Make a well in the centre, pour in the yeast mixture and the remainder of the milk and work with your hands until a sticky dough forms.
3. Tip the dough out onto a lightly floured surface and knead for 5 minutes or until it is smooth and elastic in texture.
4. Place the dough in a lightly oiled bowl, cover with a damp tea towel and leave to rise for 1 hour, or until it has doubled in size.
5. Knock back the dough, then knead it for a further 2–3 minutes on a lightly floured surface. Press the pears and half the flaked almonds into the surface of the bread, then knead or chafe until they are evenly distributed throughout the dough.

6. Flatten the dough into a round shape, then make deep cuts in the surface with a sharp knife to form a criss-cross pattern. Scatter the remaining flaked almonds over the surface. Place the dough on a greased baking tray, cover with a damp tea towel and leave to prove for 1 hour, or until it has doubled in size.

7. Preheat the oven to 180°C/ 350°F/gas mark 4.

8. Bake the loaf in the preheated oven for 25–30 minutes, or until it has risen and is golden brown. Test by tapping the base – the loaf will sound hollow when it is cooked.

9. Cool the loaf on a wire rack. Using a spoon, drizzle the melted chocolate over the top before serving.

VARIATIONS

Try substituting apples, apricots or figs for the pears and replacing the flaked almonds with chopped walnuts. The variations are limitless – just feel confident in your choices and use anything you fancy.

DATE & APPLE BREAD

This is quick, easy bread is a wonderful combination of apple and dates, mixed with spices.

INGREDIENTS *Makes 1 loaf*
250g/9oz self-raising flour
1 tsp salt
½ tsp cinnamon
¼ tsp ground nutmeg
85g/3oz butter
150g/5½oz sugar
2 eggs
90ml/3fl oz milk
175g/6oz dates, chopped
2 apples, peeled, cored
    and chopped

METHOD

1. Preheat the oven to 180°C/ 350°C/gas mark 4. Grease and lightly flour a 450g/1lb loaf tin.
2. Sift the flour into a large bowl with the salt, cinnamon and nutmeg.
3. In a bowl, cream the butter with the sugar until the mixture is light and fluffy. Add the eggs one at a time, beating well between each addition.
4. Fold the flour and the milk alternately into the creamed mixture until you have a nice smooth consistency.
5. Carefully fold in the dates and chopped apple.
6. Turn the mixture into the prepared loaf tin and bake in the preheated oven for 1¼ hours, or until a skewer inserted in the centre comes out clean.
7. Leave the loaf in the tin to cool for 10 minutes, then turn out onto a wire rack to cool completely.

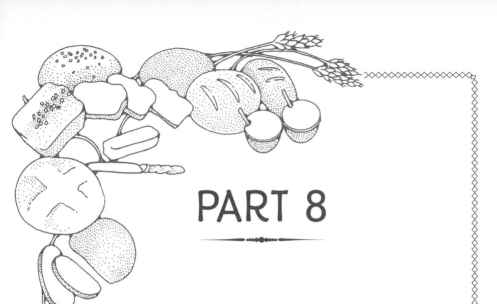

PART 8

USING UP LEFTOVERS

You don't need to throw away stale bread because there are so many ways of turning it into a new dish without much effort. For example, you could make croutons to go with your homemade soup; or how about savoury breadcrumbs or a bread and butter pudding? Any leftover crumbs can be put out on the bird table.

WASTE NOT, WANT NOT

After the love and care you have put into making your bread, it would be a pity to waste it by throwing it away once it is past the peak of its freshness.

You can do many things with bread, even if it has gone a bit stale. This section contains plenty of ideas about how to put leftovers to good use.

By far the most versatile role for leftover bread is as breadcrumbs, which are often called for in recipes. It is important to note whether the ingredients list states 'dry' or 'fresh' breadcrumbs, since the two are not interchangeable.

For dry breadcrumbs, all you need to do is put slices of bread in a low oven until they are crisp. Then place them in a large, strong freezer bag, seal it and crush with a rolling pin. For a faster method, blitz the dried bread in a food processor instead. The dried breadcrumbs can be stored in an airtight container or in the freezer. If the recipe asks for fresh breadcrumbs, simply break up slices of day-old bread and blend them in a food processor until you have even-sized crumbs. To give flavour, the breadcrumbs can be mixed with fresh herbs, chillies, Parmesan cheese, or even spices for sweet recipes.

With a little imagination, leftover bread can easily be turned into a new recipe – either sweet or savoury. For example, try bread and butter pudding with a dollop of fresh cream; cold bread pudding as part of a packed lunch; bruschetta topped with sliced tomatoes, olives and a little garlic; herby croutons to accompany a bowl of soup; or a mouthwatering apple and caramel pudding. The possibilities for the exciting use of leftovers are endless.

BRUSCHETTA WITH TOMATO & BASIL

Bruschetta are slices of rustic bread that have been toasted, rubbed with garlic and olive oil and topped with a savoury treat. In Italy these are usually served as an appetizer, but they can also be used to accompany soups.

INGREDIENTS *Makes 24 slices*

FOR THE TOPPING:
6 ripe plum tomatoes
2 garlic cloves, finely chopped
1 tbsp extra virgin olive oil
1 tsp balsamic vinegar
10 fresh basil leaves, chopped
salt and freshly ground
   black pepper

FOR THE BRUSCHETTA:
1 baguette (page 46) or ciabatta
   (page 92), cut into 24 slices
1 garlic clove, halved
60ml/2fl oz extra virgin olive oil

METHOD

1. Put the tomatoes in boiling water for 1 minute. Drain, allow to cool a little and then, using a small, sharp knife, remove the skins. Cut the tomatoes into quarters and remove the seeds and core. Chop the tomatoes finely and put them in a bowl. Add the garlic, olive oil, vinegar and basil. Season to taste with salt and pepper and set aside.

2. Preheat your grill. Score the bread slices lightly with the point of knife to make a criss-cross pattern. Toast them under the preheated grill until they are brown. (They may be cooked on a griddle instead, if you prefer a slightly charred appearance.)

3. While the bread is still hot, rub the surface with the garlic halves and drizzle with olive oil.

4. Spread the tomato topping on each slice. Put under the grill for another 2 minutes, then serve at once.

BREAD & BUTTER PUDDING

A queen among puddings, properly made bread and butter pudding is moist and fruity. It is traditionally made with raisins, but this one is adjusted slightly to use dates. You might find you can't wait for your bread to go stale before making the next one!

INGREDIENTS *Serves 4–6*
60g/2oz stoned dates, chopped
3 tbsp freshly squeezed
   orange juice
200ml/7fl oz whole milk
1 vanilla pod, halved
zest of ½ orange
75g/2½oz butter, diced
8 slices of slightly stale white
   bread, cut into triangles
3 eggs
2 tbsp caster sugar
100ml/3½fl oz double cream
1 tbsp demerara sugar
freshly grated nutmeg

METHOD
1. Put the dates into a small bowl with the orange juice, cover with a piece of cling film and leave to soak for a few hours or overnight.
2. Put the milk and vanilla pod into a small saucepan and bring to a simmer. Remove from the heat, add the orange zest and set aside until the mixture has cooled to room temperature.
3. Grease a shallow ovenproof dish (about 30cm × 20cm/12in × 8in) with butter. Generously butter the slices of bread and arrange them in the dish, overlapping them like fish scales.
4. Beat the eggs with the sugar until they are well mixed. Remove the vanilla pod from the milk. Gradually beat the milk and cream into the egg mixture to form a smooth custard.
5. Pour half the egg and milk mixture over the bread in the baking dish. Drain the dates, arrange over the top of the bread and leave for 20 minutes.

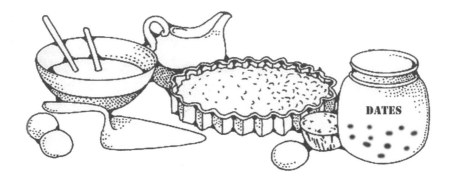

6. Preheat the oven to 180°C/ 350°F/gas mark 4.

7. Arrange the remaining bread slices to make a second layer in the baking dish. Drizzle over the remainder of the custard and dot with butter. Sprinkle the top with demerara sugar and grated nutmeg.

8. Place the baking dish inside a large roasting tin and fill halfway with water to make a *bain-marie*. Cook in the preheated oven for 35–45 minutes or until the top is golden brown.

9. Allow to stand for 10 minutes before serving with some whipped cream or custard.

NEED TO KNOW

A *bain-marie*, otherwise known as a water bath or double boiler, is used to create moisture and keep ingredients at a controlled temperature. With this method, the food being cooked is surrounded by a gentle heat. It's ideal for melting chocolate or for delicate dishes such as custard or white sauce.

BREAD PUDDING

This is another excellent way of using up stale bread, either white or wholemeal. It is more like a cake than a pudding, and is excellent served hot or cold in lunch boxes or for picnics.

INGREDIENTS *Serves 6–8*

500g/1lb 2oz stale white or
    wholemeal bread
500g/1lb 2 oz mixed dried fruit
85g/3oz dates, chopped
1½ tsp mixed spice
600ml/1pt milk
2 large eggs, beaten
140g/5oz light muscovado sugar
zest of 1 lemon
100g/3½oz butter, melted
2 tbsp demerara sugar

METHOD

1. Tear the bread into pieces and place in a mixing bowl. Add the mixed fruit, dates and spice. Pour in the milk, then scrunch the mixture with your fingers until everything is completely mixed and the bread has broken up.

2. Add the beaten eggs, muscovado sugar and lemon zest. Stir well and then set aside for 20 minutes to soak.

3. Preheat the oven to 180°C/ 350°F/gas mark 4. Butter and line the base of a 20cm/8in square cake tin.

4. Stir the melted butter into the bread mixture, pour it into the tin, then shake demerara sugar over the surface.

5. Bake in the preheated oven for 1–1½ hours or until firm and golden. If the surface starts to become too brown, cover it with some kitchen foil. Test after 1 hour by pushing a skewer into the centre. If it comes out clean then the cake is ready. If it comes out with some uncooked mixture on it then continue to bake for another 15–30 minutes.

6. Serve hot as a pudding with custard, or sliced cold as a cake.

CROUTONS

Home-made croutons are so easy to make and a real treat when floated on top of soup or as a crunchy addition to liven up a salad.

INGREDIENTS *Makes about 30*
115g/4oz white bread
3 tbsp olive oil

METHOD
1. Preheat the oven to 180°C/ 350°F/gas mark 4.
2. Cut 2 slices of bread, about 2cm/¾in thick. Remove the crusts and cut into 2cm/¾in cubes.
3. Pour the olive oil into a bowl, add the bread cubes and toss them with your hands until they are completely coated in oil. Leave to stand for 5 minutes so the bread absorbs the oil.
4. Spread the bread cubes out on a baking tray, allowing a little space between each one. Place in the preheated oven and cook for 5 minutes.
5. Remove the croutons from the oven, turn them over and cook for another 5 minutes. Keep an eye on them towards the end of the cooking time as they may go brown quite quickly and you need to take care they do not burn. The croutons are ready when they are golden brown.

VARIATIONS

If you are serving onion soup, make a larger version of these croutons and melt some gruyère or Cheddar cheese on top before floating in the soup. For tomato soup, add some chopped parsley or basil to the oil. For a change use some chilli oil to add a little kick to your croutons.

CARAMEL APPLE PUDDING

This pudding can be made with any type of day-old bread and will melt in your mouth.

INGREDIENTS *Serves 8*

60g/2oz butter, plus extra for greasing

6 eating apples, peeled and cored

1 tbsp lemon juice

½ tsp ground cinnamon

100g/3½oz brown sugar

75g/2½oz raisins

200g/7oz day-old white bread, cut into 5cm/2in pieces

2 eggs, plus 2 egg yolks

250ml/8fl oz milk

1 tsp vanilla essence

½ tsp freshly grated nutmeg

METHOD

1. Preheat the oven to 180°C/ 350°F/gas mark 4. Generously grease a shallow baking dish (28cm× 18cm × 4cm/11in × 7in × 1½in) with butter.

2. Cut the prepared apples into 1cm/½in slices. Put the apple pieces in a large mixing bowl, add the lemon juice and cinnamon and set aside.

3. Melt the butter and half the brown sugar in a heavy-based frying pan over medium heat. Stir in the apple mixture using a wooden spoon and cook, stirring frequently, until the apples are soft and beginning to turn golden brown. This should take about 10–15 minutes. Stir in the raisins, transfer the mixture to a large bowl and leave to cool.

4. Place the bread pieces on baking trays and toast in the preheated oven until crisp.

5. Place half the apple mixture in the baking dish. Add the toasted bread to the remaining apples in the bowl and stir well to combine. Spoon the mixture over the top of the apples already in the dish.

6. In a separate bowl, combine

the eggs, egg yolks, milk, remaining brown sugar, vanilla essence and nutmeg and whisk until the sugar has dissolved and the mixture is light and fluffy – this should take about 2 minutes.

7. Pour the egg mixture evenly over the apple and bread mixture and leave it to soak for about 10–15 minutes, or until the bread has absorbed all of the liquid.

8. Bake in the centre of the preheated oven for about 45–50 minutes, or until it is puffed up and golden brown on top.

9. Serve hot with some cream.

FRENCH TOAST

For a really quick and delicious breakfast, try some French toast drizzled with maple syrup and topped with a sliced banana.

INGREDIENTS *Makes 2 slices*

1 egg, beaten
1 tbsp milk
½ tsp ground cinnamon
2 slices of day-old bread about
  1cm/½in thick
oil and butter, for frying

METHOD

1. Beat the egg with the milk in a bowl that is large enough to accommodate the bread too, then stir in the ground cinnamon.

2. Soak the bread in the egg mixture and leave for 5 minutes or until it has absorbed most of the liquid.

3. Heat a little oil and butter in a heavy-based frying pan until it is hot but not smoking.

4. Fry the slices of bread for about 2 minutes on each side or until they have gone golden brown. Serve warm, drizzled with maple syrup and topped with slices of banana.

INDEX

Anise crown bread 75
Baking stones 93
Banana and courgette bread 133
Banana bread, gluten-free 106
Bannocks 96
Bara brith 116
Beer bread with honey 68
Black pepper and fig bread 80
Black pepper flat bread 91
Bread and butter pudding 152–153
Bread pudding 154
Brioche 120
Brown soda bread, gluten-free 108
Bruschetta with tomato and basil 151
Calzone 84–85
Caramel apple pudding 156–157
Carrot and raisin muffins 121
Cheese and onion rolls 70–71
Cheese and potato rolls 72
Chelsea buns 124–125
Chocolate chip muffins 131
Ciabatta 92–93
Ciabatta, gluten-free 104
Classics, The
    classic white loaf 39
    cottage loaf 48–49
    french stick 46–47
    granary loaf 42–43
    Irish soda bread 58
    milk loaf 52–53
    mixed seed loaf 56–57
    rustic rye bread 54–55
    rye breadsticks 55
    soft white dinner rolls 44–45
    sourdough bread 50–51
    wholemeal loaf 40–41
Classic white loaf 39

Cornbread 63
Cottage loaf 48–49
Croutons 155
Crumpets, gluten-free 105
Date and apple bread 148
Date and walnut rolls 62
Date loaf 114–115
    no-yeast version 115
Doughnuts 134–135
Dutch apple bread 130
Equipment
    baking moulds and tins 21
    baking parchment 22
    electric mixer 21
    knife 22
    measuring cups and spoons 20
    pastry brushes 22
    proving bowls or tubs 22
    scales 19
    scrapers 21
    tea towel 22
    US cups 20
    wire cooling rack 22
Fats 18
Flat breads
    bannocks 96
    black pepper flat bread 91
    calzone 84–85
    ciabatta 92–93
    focaccia 86–87
    Mexican tortillas 90
    naan bread 89
    pitta bread 88
    pizza dough 83
    potato flat bread 98
    rosemary and garlic flat bread 97
    rôti 94

rye crispbread 95
Flour
    buckwheat 12–13
    corn 13
    granary 11–12
    oatmeal 13
    plain flour 12
    rye 13
    self-raising 12
    spelt 13, 74
    stoneground 12
    strong 12
    wheat 11
    wheatmeal 12
    wholemeal 12
Focaccia, classic 86–87
French stick, classic 46-47
French toast 157
Gingerbread 132
Gluten 11, 12, 13, 17
Gluten-free breads
    banana bread 106
    brown soda bread 108
    ciabatta 104
    crumpets 105
    honey and sunflower seed loaf 109
    linseed, date and raisin bread 110
    marmalade breakfast loaf 107
    pizza base 102–103
    pizza toppings 103
    sandwich loaf 101
Granary loaf 42–43
Herby plait 76–77
Honey and sunflower seed loaf, gluten-
    free 109
Hot cross buns 122–123
Hydration 16
Irish soda bread 58
Lardy cake 128–129
Lemon and blueberry bread 145
Lemon and lavender bread 113
Linseed, date and raisin bread, gluten-
    free 110

Liquids 17
Luxury fruit scones 118–119
Marmalade breakfast loaf, gluten-free
    107
Mexican tortillas 90
Milk loaf 52–53
Mixed seed loaf 56–57
Naan bread 89
Olive and rosemary bread 61
Olives 61, 78–79
Olive swirls 78–79
Panettone 140–141
Parmesan and courgette bread 66–67
Pear and almond bread 146–147
Pitta bread 88
Pizza base, gluten-free 102–103
Pizza dough 83
Pizza toppings, gluten-free 103
Potato flat bread 98
Prune and chocolate bread 138–139
Pumpernickel 65
Pumpkin bread 136
Quick and sweet breads
    banana and courgette bread 133
    bara brith 116
    brioche 120
    carrot and raisin muffins 121
    Chelsea buns 124–125
    chocolate chip muffins 131
    date and apple bread 148
    date loaf 114–115
    doughnuts 134–135
    Dutch apple bread 130
    gingerbread 132
    hot cross buns 122–123
    lardy cake 128–129
    lemon and blueberry bread 145
    lemon and lavender bread 113
    luxury fruit scones 118–119
    panettone 140–141
    pear and almond bread 146–147
    prune and chocolate bread 138–139
    pumpkin bread 136

Sally Lunn 144
savoury scones 117
sticky malt loaf 127
stollen 142–143
tea cakes 137
waffles 126
Raising agents
chemical 16
sourdough starter 15
yeast 13–14
Rosemary and garlic flat bread 97
Rôti 94
Rustic rye bread 54–55
Rye and crème fraîche bread 64
Rye breadsticks 55
Rye crispbread 95
Sally Lunn 144
Salt 16
Sandwich loaf, gluten-free 101
Savoury scones 117
Soft white dinner rolls 44–45
Sourdough bread 50–51
Speciality breads
anise crown bread 75
beer bread with honey 68
black pepper and fig bread 80
cheese and onion rolls 70–71
cheese and potato rolls 72
cornbread 63
date and walnut rolls 62
herby plait 76–77
olive and rosemary bread 61
olive swirls 78–79
parmesan and courgette bread 66–67
pumpernickel 65
rye and crème fraîche bread 64
sun-dried tomato bread 69
spelt bread 74
tiger bread 73
Spelt bread 74
Sticky malt loaf 127
Stollen 142–143
Sugar 17–18

Sun-dried tomato bread 69
Tea cakes 137
Techniques
baking 32
final stages 33
steam 32
baking stones 93
chafing 27–28
glazes and toppings 32
kneading 25
firm dough 26
soft dough 26
knocking back 29
preparation 24
mixing 24–25
proving 31
rising 28
shaping 29
cottage loaf 30
long 30
oval 30
plait 30, 76–77
rolls 30
round 29
storing and freezing 33
stretch test 27
Tiger bread 73
Tomato sauce 82
Troubleshooting 34–36
Using up leftovers
bread and butter pudding 152–153
bread pudding 154
bruschetta with tomato and basil 151
caramel apple pudding 156–157
croutons 155
french toast 157
Waffles 126
Wholemeal loaf 40–41
Yeast
dried 14
easy-blend 14
fresh 14–15